The Complete Book of
FURNITURE RESTORATION

The Complete Book of
FURNITURE
RESTORATION

Tristan Salazar

TIGER BOOKS INTERNATIONAL
LONDON
A Bison Book

This edition published by
Tiger Books International Ltd.
London.

Produced by
Bison Books Ltd.
176 Old Brompton Road,
London, SW5 0BA
England

ISBN 1-870461-47-9

Printed in Hong Kong

Reprinted 1988

AUTHOR'S NOTE
Some of the processes and chemicals used in this book are potentially extremely
dangerous. Great care should be taken, and manufacturer's instructions followed
at all times.

For Ruth

CONTENTS

INTRODUCTION

If you are good with your hands and have a basic understanding of wood, then restoration is well within your capabilities. Much of it is simply a matter of common sense, patience and, of course, experience. Unfortunately at least half the good quality furniture that comes into the restorer's workshop has suffered from bad repairs. Consequently, it is with some hesitation that any professional restorer takes on the task of explaining his craft through words and photographs. The problem lies not in a misunderstanding of the techniques, but in how they should be applied in practice. Each piece of furniture has its own problems that sometimes cannot be covered by a set pattern of instructions. However, you have to start somewhere! First accept that there is a correct and an incorrect way of restoring furniture. I have tried to emphasize throughout this book the necessity of applying the simple principles of restoration to any piece of furniture, irrespective of its date. By starting out on modern and twentieth-century pieces, with restoration as opposed to repair in mind and by continually conserving as much of the original as possible, it becomes so much easier for the enthusiast to graduate with experience to restoring the more valuable and older types of furniture. The difference between restoring the old and the new piece is marginal. The former requires the continual awareness of how furniture improves with age and how you have to cater for these effects of time. Modern pieces rarely exhibit these characteristics, but it is important to carry out repairs with the same basic principle in mind. The cost of modern furniture and the escalating pace of life has resulted in an increasing appreciation of the furniture of yesterday.

Restoration is a fascinating craft involving subjects ranging from furniture history, cabinetmaking, basic chemistry, metal work and color sense to a knowledge of timber species and how they work in furniture. Such a diversity of both subjects and problems compensates for the fact that in all restoration work it is necessary to subjugate personal preference and choose parts in keeping with the style. In restoration you are constantly adapting to someone else's work and methods and you rarely find the kind of return you would expect from making your own furniture. Hours can be spent in repairing a groundwork which eventually has to have its veneer returned. A well-restored piece should look as if it had been well-kept all its life.

I have tried to cover as much ground as possible in this small volume without spreading the information too thinly. The acquiring furniture section should start you off in being able to recognize the forms to be found in antique and reproduction furniture while the tools and wood sections cover the materials you might find useful. Basic constructional repairs and their peculiarities to certain shapes are dealt with in the chapters on chairs, tables and cabinets. Metal work, surface and finish restoration completes an overall picture and the allied subjects of upholstery, caning, rush work and wicker are dealt with in the finishing stages.

I have included a brief historical introduction to the various techniques and crafts to be found in restoration. Hopefully these will help you to get the feel of the piece you are restoring. I find that knowing when and why certain techniques were used is an integral part of restoration. An understanding of the history of the techniques makes the task of dealing with an unfamiliar piece of furniture far less daunting. Hopefully this book should put you on the right track, but it is experience that always proves to be the best guide.

Opposite top: A room in Art Nouveau style, as featured in Liberty's exhibition at the Victoria and Albert Museum, London. Opposite, below: A reconstruction of a typical 1930s living room. Exhibits like this give an impression of how furniture would have looked at its time of construction.

ACQUIRING FURNITURE

With the increasing cost of furniture, whether it is antique or modern, buying damaged pieces and restoring them is a good way of forming an inexpensive but good-quality collection. The more experience one has in restoration work, the easier it becomes to spot a bargain. Furniture can look appalling when it is dirty and damaged. What might appear to be a wreck of a table to the uninitiated, for example, can often prove a straightforward job to someone with a modicum of workshop experience.

How to buy furniture

The best advice to the newcomer to restoration is to select well-made modern pieces that are pleasing to the eye. Badly made furniture of whatever date is difficult to restore and is best left to those who have

been in the field a bit longer. Avoid starting work on antique pieces; at the end of the day if you have made a few mistakes at least you will not have wasted your money by ruining a valuable item.

Moving on from the 'buy what you like' principle, an appreciation of the styles peculiar to certain periods can be of great help. While books and photographs outline these styles, you cannot beat the practical experience of viewing furniture in museums and collections. Here you can see how old wood, finishes and techniques ought to appear in relation to certain periods and styles. Obviously you would be very lucky to come across these top-quality pieces in salerooms and shops, but at least they will help you to distinguish between the antique, fake and reproduction.

It is very instructive to watch how the expert goes about buying furniture. Good dealers stand back and look at the piece as a whole, relying heavily on their first impressions. Only when satisfied that the piece looks right do they inspect the details, joints and finishes to make sure that they confirm the original summary. To get involved in the details of a piece straight away usually results in an inability to distinguish the wood from the trees. Furniture embellishments such as florid carvings and fancy moldings can be extremely distracting.

Below: Antique shops can be good places to pick up bargains. Rankine Taylor Antiques, Cirencester, is laid out to resemble a room.

Places to buy furniture

Secondhand and junk shops are good places for acquiring the odd bargain. Among the piles of uninteresting furniture there often lingers a well-made piece that is worth resurrecting. Since these shops operate on the principle that everything and anything will sell eventually, they are good places for buying bits of furniture, old tools and parts of table tops for use in restoration. Antique shops sell furniture that is in good condition or already restored, so they are not generally ideal places to acquire pieces for repair.

Salerooms and auction houses provide the best hunting ground for the restorer with a degree of experience. Many damaged pieces come up for sale, sometimes untouched by previous repair work. Unfortunately you are on your own when it comes to the bidding so it is imperative to check the goods thoroughly. Not all auction houses are infallible in their cataloguing of items for sale. Those useful and nebulous tags of 'antique' and 'country' are tied to many dubious pieces that seem to defy any other form of classification. When buying at auctions, try to establish the top price you are willing to pay before starting to bid. Auction fever is very catching and can lead to excessive prices.

Furniture categories

Before dealing with a brief summary of the various furniture styles a word or two has to be said about some of the broad and sometimes confusing terms used in the trade for grouping furniture.

Country Furniture This is a generic term often used to cover a multitude of sins. In the antique trade, the label of country is applied to pieces of furniture that were made in the provinces as opposed to the capitals. Most of these types reflect the fashionable designs of the cities and were turned out in the provincial urban workshops which catered to the less well-off of their clients by using cheap local woods such as ash and oak rather than expensive and imported varieties such as mahogany and satinwood. At its best country furniture, whether made in the country or the town, is superb – it is well made from good-quality timber and designed to last. Dating and attribution can be difficult with country furniture but are nearly impossible with primitive or farmhouse furniture. These rustic types have become immensely popular both in the United States and England because they are so far removed from our uniform and machine age. Being utilitarian and of no apparent school of design, they could belong to any period and so supplement the dwindling stocks of antique furniture. Old farm benches and stools which were made for practical purposes only 50 or so years ago can, and very often do, take on the appearance of a 200-year-old antique. The amount of wear and tear and natural polishing they are exposed to gives them a great degree of 'age' and superb patination. The age of these pieces is often irrelevant as they have a naive charm of their own; however do not pay seventeenth-century prices for what could well be a slab of twentieth-century wood.

Above: An eighteenth-century country dresser.
Left: A mid-seventeenth century Dutch farmhouse interior. Detail of an engraving after Adriaen Van Ostade (1610–1684). 'Farmhouse' furniture is difficult to date as it was primarily designed for practical purposes. Except for the three-legged stool designed to cope with uneven flagstones and earthen floors, this type of furniture was made between 1600 and 1900. Note the slab-top table (right), the rush-seated chair (center) and part of a food cupboard (top left).

Antique Furniture The term 'antique' recently has become somewhat hazy in definition. In theory it should only encompass objects which were made over 100 years ago. However, with the scarcity of good-quality furniture predating 1880, many antique shops have lowered their sights and found a ready market for well-constructed and decorative pieces from the 1920s and the art deco period. These 'antiques of tomorrow,' can prove a wiser investment than the multitude of badly made pieces produced from the 1860s onward. At the other end of the scale there are still a few shops who refuse to touch anything made after 1830, restricting themselves solely to what is known as 'period' furniture.

While the usual definition now rests at 1880, for ease of reference in this book, the antique period will end in the mid-nineteenth century. This might seem an arbitrary choice but it marks the point at which factory-line and mass-production techniques really began to dominate the market, particularly in North America. Prior to this date the majority of furniture was handmade.

Furniture classified as antique is not automatically good quality. Badly constructed pieces can be found as far back as the seventeenth century. Schlock and Borax are American terms for badly made furniture of any period or date, and have helped to destroy the myth that things were better made in the old days. Unfortunately this misleading concept still surfaces now and again because time often obscures shoddy workmanship and appalling carpentry can be excused as being rustic, quaint or country. Antique furniture, even if badly made, is still expensive. It encapsulates bygone methods of

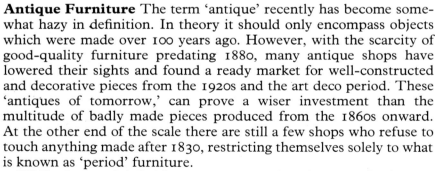

Right: The Lee Priory Room, known as the 'Strawberry Room,' is English, circa 1783. Many pieces of furniture were designed as part of an overall scheme, particularly during the eighteenth century. A lot can be learned about furniture by visiting collections.

construction and consequently should be restored with all the care and attention that would be lavished on a well-made antique. Beginners should avoid it like the plague, it can prove very trying.

An outline of furniture history and styles

A summary of 350 years of British, French and American furniture, for reasons of brevity, has to be rather general in nature. Much of the furniture you are likely to encounter belongs to the nineteenth century and modern period but it is important to go a little further back in time to understand furniture styles and techniques. The earliest pieces that can still be had relatively cheaply date from about 1630 and their restoration is best undertaken after a few years of constant practical experience. Pieces that have been around for 200 years or so naturally show signs of wear that become part of the piece and are accepted by collectors as such. Removing dents and scratches from early furniture destroys the value of the antique, so if you do come across furniture that is valuable, always consult the expert. It can be a lot cheaper to pay a professional restorer than to attempt to restore it yourself.

When viewing the confusing scene of furniture history three main points can be useful. First, with our acceptance of modern materials such as the laminates and plys with which even the worst kind of handyman can build furniture, it is frequently ignored that many early designs were dictated by the varying characteristics and technical limitations of solid wood. Very often designs were born out of the characteristics of the timbers used. The Jacobean panelled coffer was designed to cope with the fact that wood shrinks considerably in dry conditions and expands in wet, a particular problem with large solid areas of wood. To overcome this problem the early craftsman set the thin areas of panelling in unglued rabbets so that they could move freely without tearing themselves or the construction apart. This arrangement also made the furniture lighter in appearance and weight. New techniques and materials freed the craftsman from these limitations so that design became more a reflection of his personality as opposed to that of the material.

Second, it can be useful to regard each of the main styles as a development of or reaction against the previous style. Hepplewhite furniture, for instance, shows a return to simplicity and elegance after the elaborate neoclassical furniture of Robert Adam while at the same time still employing many classical motifs. A simplistic way of looking at styles is to view them as alternating between being fussy and being simple. Queen Anne furniture of the early 1700s is a total change from the elaborate furniture of the late 1600s and was replaced by yet another busy type – rococo. This too was ousted in favor of the more severe lines and shapes of the neoclassical period and so it went on until the Victorian period, where you find some of the most elaborate furniture ever designed. Today simplicity is favored, hence the popularity of country furniture and colonial types.

Third, furniture styles are inextricably linked with the social attitudes and economic stability of the various countries. To view them as part of history and as a reflection of the current attitudes can be of great help. Mid- to late Victorian furniture seems to sum up all the pomp and fragile self-assurance of its era.

The dates of the various styles should only be seen as a general guide, as designs and techniques overlap from one period into the next. Similarly, beware of the labels that furniture is given in antique shops as named furniture sells better. Terms like Phyffe, Sheraton,

Below: An Italian walnut armchair from the mid-seventeenth century. Stamped on the back of the carved front stretcher is 'GVIBERD★ HONNORAT.' Although rare, it is always worth looking for an inventory, maker's or trade mark on furniture. This one is an owner's mark made during a household inventory.

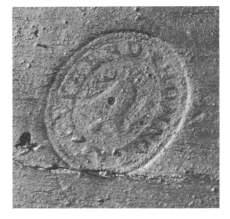

Hepplewhite and Chippendale are extremely elastic and do not necessarily mean that the piece belongs to its period or comes from the cabinet shops of the named craftsmen.

Developments in America, although revealing many traits peculiar to the USA, basically follow the course of European and English design. An appraisal of the English scene includes much of what was happening across the Atlantic. A few differences occur in the following way:

One/English furniture is often labelled according to the most fashionable wood in use. There is the age of oak (1500–1660), the age of walnut (1660–1730) and the age of mahogany (1730–1825). Such general distinctions are not so easy to apply to American furniture. The early colonial carpenter, for example, made use of any wood that came to hand. Maple, walnut, pine, hickory and birch offered him a far wider scope and ease of working than did oak. Consequently his designs show a flowing and curved nature, borne out of the pliable characteristics of some of these woods. In the mid- and late-eighteenth century, the English craftsman was enjoying an abundant supply of imported mahogany, his fellow American supplemented his small stock with cherrywood. Furniture from this period is often made of this so-called 'American mahogany.'

Two/The dissemination of European patterns through the colonies was a slow process owing to the primitive means of communication and travel. Not only did designs arrive at a later date but many forms which had long gone out of fashion in Europe were retained for longer periods in America. This time lag closed up as the means of communication improved but even so the American craftsman was not quite as susceptible to fashion as his European cousin. He adopted and altered designs that were practical and pleasing and stuck with them. Consequently although the 'William and Mary' style can be said to end in England in 1700, it continued in various forms in Pennsylvania, New Jersey and Connecticut well into the 1700s.

Three/In Europe country furniture and urban varieties have been regarded as separate classes of furniture. The carpenter, joiner and turner belonged to the provinces while the aristocrat of the trade, the cabinetmaker, worked in the main capitals. These branches rarely overlapped and each man stuck to his particular trade. However, the American craftsman disregarded such restrictions. For example, he developed the country Windsor chair into a sophisticated urban variety. As late as the 1760s some forms of urban American furniture still show the carpenter's hand at work. American Chippendale chairs are sometimes joined with the carpenter's mortise and tenon, a method of fixing that was never used in the urban cabinetmaking shops of eighteenth-century England.

Jacobean

This loose term is used to cover a style that was prevalent in England and the colonies throughout the main part of the seventeenth century. While all sorts of woods were used in America, until 1660 much English furniture was made from oak. Pieces are recognizable by their square and heavy construction. The box shape predominates in joined stools, small tables, cupboards and solid wooden chairs and armchairs, mostly made by carpenters and joiners. Joiners used dry mortise and tenon joints secured by a wooden peg and attempted to hide the method of construction. Carpenters made utilitarian furniture so did not always avoid using nails or cover up joint work. Decoration in the Jacobean style usually takes the form of shallow carving, scratched moldings and applied split turnings.

Above: A Chinese Chippendale chair, circa 1760.

Below: A Jacobean-style chair from the first half of the seventeenth century.

Restoration period (1660–1689)

The restoration of the monarchy to England in 1660 brought with it a total change from traditional methods of construction and decoration. The continental craftsmen brought back by Charles II after his exile abroad and the great fire of London in 1666 helped bring about a refreshing change. The fire of London destroyed much old oak furniture and with it the inherent traditions. The market was now open for the foreign craftsmen to exercise their skills. In London oak was used only for the unseen parts of furniture while walnut became the fashionable wood. The new techniques of cabinetmaking – veneering, caning and lacquer work – enhanced the appearance of furniture. New types of furniture appeared, such as the chest of drawers. Chairs became more sophisticated and taller in their backs. Overall, the Restoration was a period of joyful exuberance in design, a celebration of the return of the monarchy after the dour puritanism of the Commonwealth period. Although the age of the cabinetmaker had begun and the new techniques and forms were used to the full in the capital, they had little immediate effect on country furniture or pieces in the colonies.

Top: Chair backs became taller during the last two decades of the seventeenth century. Above: Curvilinear forms and a restrained decoration denote Queen Anne and early Georgian styles.

Left: A walnut chair from the Charles II period (1660–1685). The square shape of the Jacobean period is still retained.

William and Mary (1689–1702)

The furniture designs of this period, while still under the influence of the continental craftsmen, control the excesses of the Restoration Period. It was a stage of transformation, so to speak, from the elaborate shapes toward the simpler forms of the Queen Anne style. In England walnut continued to be used and the furniture of this period is characterized by the use of marquetry, lacquer work and the scroll and large turned leg for chests and chests on stands.

Left: An English side table from the William and Mary period.

American Colonial (1630–1700)

Apart from practical considerations, colonial furniture of this period often uses motifs and other decorations from the mother countries. Pennsylvania, for example, was originally settled by the Swiss and Germans so furniture produced in these settlements shows peculiarities such as scrolls and painted decoration. The Connecticut carved-oak chest, with its use of shallow carving and applied split spindles, owes much to seventeenth-century England. Overall, early colonial furniture, although heavy in construction, has an appearance of lightness that is lacking in European examples, partly because painting was used to enhance the carving and design.

Queen Anne (1702–1714)

The eighteenth century is often called the golden age of cabinet-making. Admittedly some fine examples were made in this period but as far as craftsmanship goes, good-quality furniture from the 1800s is just as well made. The eighteenth century was a period of consolidation of the arts in general, particularly in England where a strong emphasis was laid on trying to establish a national or particularly British style. England has always acted as a kind of restraining filter through which elaborate designs from the continent have been sieved and passed on to North America in a simplified form.

Alongside the Windsor chair, Shaker furniture and art and crafts pieces, Queen Anne furniture encapsulates all that is best in design –

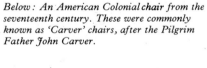

Below: An American Colonial chair from the seventeenth century. These were commonly known as 'Carver' chairs, after the Pilgrim Father John Carver.

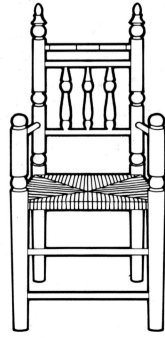

a simple and careful balance of form and material. Decoration is kept to a minimum and the natural beauty of walnut is allowed to speak for itself. The whole Queen Anne style can be best seen in a chair of this period. Here you have a beautiful balance of contrasting curves and curvilinear forms, echoed in the shape of the cabriole leg. The stretcher used in the previous period for joining legs was removed and the back of the chair consists of the shaped uprights with a central broad splat leading up to the hooped cresting tail. Two new innovations appear during this period – the drop-in or insert seat and a type of folding-top card table. Although the elegant cabriole leg had been introduced from Holland in about 1690, in this period it began to loose its original square-sectioned form and take on the shape familiar today.

Left: An English walnut chair, circa 1730. Here the carved cabriole leg is fully developed and terminates in a claw and ball foot. Although this chair belongs to the early Georgian period, it still retains much of the earlier era, associated with the Queen Anne style. Reproductions based on this form are usually termed Queen Anne.

Below: A typical Queen Anne style chair.

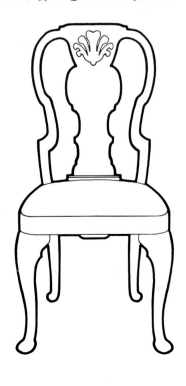

Early Georgian (1714–1740)

Furniture of this period remained fairly restrained in its basic form although embellishments started to appear in the form of carving. It could be described as a decorated form of Queen Anne. Chair backs which had had a hooped or domed shape throughout the late seventeenth century and through the Queen Anne period started to flatten out toward the Chippendale form. The most important feature of this period is the introduction of mahogany on a large scale in the 1730s. It began to replace walnut as the main wood; initially it was used in the solid and veneering was discontinued for a short period.

The fashion for tea drinking brought about two new types of furniture during the early Georgian period – the tripod and the folding-top tea table. The drop-leaf table was introduced also. It differs from the early gate leg in that the stretchers were removed and the folding top was supported by two diametrically opposite legs which pulled out and pivoted on a knuckle joint from the base.

Left : An English walnut tallboy, circa *1740.*

Below : An English chair, circa *1740. The pierced decoration of the back splat shows the influence of the French rococo style. The uprights have become vertical, losing the curvilinear forms of the Queen Anne style. The top cresting rail is no longer hooped and is flattening out toward the form associated with Chippendale.*

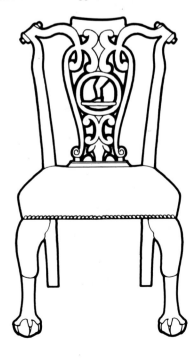

Louis XV and the Rococo style (1723–74)

Holland led the field in furniture production and design throughout the seventeenth century but during the next 100 years France became the main center for design. The Louis XV style is a generic term for furniture design which is synonymous with the rococo – a sophisticated and elegant version of the baroque. It is characterized by sweeping curves, a high degree of fancy decoration and the use of asymmetrical patterns. The rococo, or 'French taste' as it is sometimes called, had far-reaching effects on design in Europe. In Britain designers like Chippendale tempered and blended this new style into a particularly English form and it was in this modified version that the rococo eventually reached America in the 1760s. A characteristic innovation of the Louis XV period was the broad and wide open upholstered chair. It is probably one of the most popular designs for reproduction and copy furniture.

Thomas Chippendale

Chippendale is often accused of being the biggest plagiarist and overrated designer of all time. Many people consider that all he did was take the Queen Anne style and embellish it with the rococo. However, he was responsible for bringing about the birth of a uniquely English style. Admittedly his designs owe much to the previous generation but Chippendale is an unmistakable individual style. His importance rests in the fact that he was the first English cabinetmaker to publish a comprehensive pattern book that tied all the loose ends of prevailing taste such as the rococo, Gothic and Chinese into an intelligible and unique style.

Many of his rococo designs were based on his skill as a carver but an indication of his amazing ability to adapt successfully to new techniques and styles can be seen in his neoclassical period. He dropped carving altogether and fluidly changed to the use of marquetry as the main form of decoration.

Chippendale is characterized by the use of flowing lines, carving in the form of C-scrolls, floral motifs, fret work and acanthus leaves. The carved cabriole leg terminating in the claw and ball foot is another feature associated with the English rococo/Chippendale style.

Above: A Louis XV table, circa 1760.
Below left: A Louis XV chair.
Below center: The Chippendale rococo style.
Below: A Chippendale ladder-back, circa 1760.

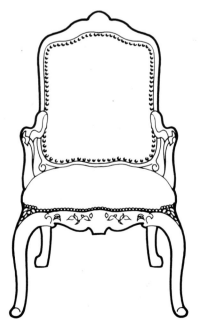

American furniture (1700–1760)

Only recently has American colonial furniture begun to be appreciated. Fancy eighteenth-century European designs seem to have dominated the American collector's taste, which is rather strange since colonial furniture often leaves it looking extremely fussy. During the first half of the 1700s America continued to follow European patterns. While the rococo was in full swing in Europe the Anglo-Dutch style still prevailed in America. Both William and Mary and Queen Anne forms remained until the 1750s and at this stage the typical American highboy or chest-on-chest appeared. The gate-leg table, long seen in Europe, took the interesting shape of the oval butterfly table. Here the open-gate arrangement was replaced by pivoting a slab of wood, shaped in the form of butterfly wings, between the top and bottom stretchers. It was often made of maple and was popular from 1700–50. Drop-leaf tables in solid cherrywood with Queen Anne-style elongated cabriole legs were also made in this period. By the 1750s the tripod table had become immensely popular in the colonies. Veneering and lacquer work began to provide an alternative to solid wood and painted decoration.

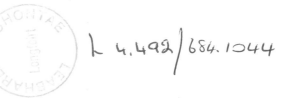

Below: The Pennsylvania Dutch room at the American Museum in Britain. The term Pennsylvania Dutch is a corruption of Deutsch (German).

The Windsor chair (1725–   )

The Windsor chair has to be considered separately because it belongs to an isolated area of design. Basically it can be considered as a sub-section of English country furniture and colonial furniture. It is one of the most successful and cheapest designs to produce. Most people associate the Windsor chair with the characteristic bentwood back and use of spindles and turned legs. However it is a very broad term, covering the type of stool-chair made from solid wood whose construction centers around the seat into which are fixed the back and legs. One of the first rules of furniture construction is to use well-seasoned timber but the Windsor chair successfully defies such a criteria. Green wood was often used because it could be bent into shape and worked with a limited amount of tools. As different woods were used for various components whose characters suited each function, a uniform effect was achieved by painting these chairs various colors. Black, green and red were the most popular.

Above: A Louis XVI chair.

Louis XVI and the first phase of neoclassicism (1774–1793)

By the 1760s the design centers of Europe, particularly France, now viewed the rococo style as being frivolous. Neoclassicism became the impetus for furniture design. Initially this style was modelled on an

Below: A Louis XVI commode.

idealistic view of ancient Rome and classical forms and is now known as the Louis XVI or Adam style (after its main exponent in England – Robert Adam). Like the rococo, neoclassicism eventually became universal. Despite the use of elaborate inlays and ormolu mounts the basic shape is rigid and square, unlike the rococo which flows all over the place. If curves are used they are pure ovals or circles, or parts of such shapes. The cabriole leg disappears and is replaced by the straight taper leg, often fluted down its length in the manner of a classical column. Apart from brass mounts and classical carving, the surface of furniture is flat and decoration takes the form of a geometrical arrangement of marquetry. By about 1800 a more serious and academic approach to classical forms was adopted in Europe although the first phase continued in America for another 10 years.

French provincial furniture (1750–1800)

Like the English joiner and carpenter, who unhurriedly adopted urban patterns and altered them to suit country living, the French provincial carpenter and cabinetmaker adapted the court patterns and styles of Louis XV. The neoclassical forms of Louis XVI did not suit the *menuisier* and he continued making a countrified version of the rococo right up until 1800. As is often the case with country furniture, designs were simplified and nonessentials removed so that the end result is often more appealing to modern taste than the original and elaborate source. The *armoire* (wardrobe) sums up French provincial, with its blunted and flattened use of rococo forms that surround and complement large areas of unadorned panelling.

Above: An Adam chair, circa 1775.

Below: A French Provincial chest of drawers with rococo pulls and typical use of blunted asymmetrical carving to the drawer fronts.

Hepplewhite (late 1700s)

George Hepplewhite's design was largely influenced by Robert Adam's neoclassical style. The difference between the two rests in the fact that Adam's furniture was largely geared toward the rich aristocrat, while Hepplewhite pieces were produced for a less affluent market. It is a domesticated version of Adam and although neoclassical in concept it is lightened by the use of the rococo. The Hepplewhite style can be characterized by light construction, serpentine shapes, the use of pale colored woods like satinwood inlaid with exotic timbers and finally the thin and tapering square leg for chairs and cabinets. The shield-back and stepped-back chair are two types associated with this style.

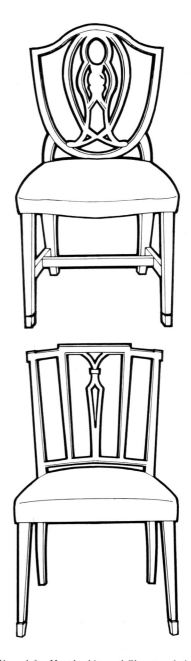

Sheraton (late 1700s)

While conceived in the same spirit as Hepplewhite, Thomas Sheraton's designs show a lighter and more angular treatment of furniture shapes. They seem far more in tune with the serious approach to adopting the forms of neoclassicism that began during the Directory in France. The style is associated with square-backed chairs, large areas of wood bordered with stringing and banding, excessively slender taper legs and reeding decoration.

French Directoire (1795–1800)

This period is a kind of bridge between the grandeur and pomp of Louis XVI and the more dignified and academic treatment of classical forms to be found in the Empire period. It tries to make a conscious break from the elaborate forms associated with the monarchy by employing a more simplified use of ornament and the revival of large areas of unadorned wood, but it still suffers from the grand designs of the preceding era. As the period of the Directory in France symbolized the birth of a new political era and the end of the monarchy it was actively encouraged by American leaders as a style that would symbolize America's own revolution. Known as 'Greek revival' in the United States, its main exponent was Duncan Phyffe, who dropped Hepplewhite and Sheraton patterns in favor of this style.

Above left: Hepplewhite and Sheraton designs can easily be confused. These Hepplewhite chairs can be recognized by their back uprights, which are not parallel.
Top: A typical Hepplewhite chair with elegant serpentine lines and pierced splat.
Above: Sheraton chairs show a thin and spidery use of classical ornament.

Above: The Greek Revival Room in the American Museum in Britain. 'Greek revival' is the second phase of the American neoclassic style. Several of the pieces in this room are attributed to Duncan Phyffe (1768–1854). Initially Phyffe worked mainly in the style of Sheraton but by about 1810 he was following the more archaeological approach to classical forms and vocabulary as used in English Regency period. He is credited as one of the main cabinetmakers of this so-called American Empire style.
Left: An English satinwood Pembroke table, late-eighteenth century. This type of small table was made from the 1780s onward. Both Hepplewhite and Sheraton are associated with this form but this example is more Sheraton in feeling.

American Federal period (1790–1830)

It is difficult to talk of a Federal style for furniture. Basically the term Federal denotes an historical period rather than a type of furniture. After the War of Independence, the main influences on American craftsmen were the English styles of Adam, Hepplewhite and Sheraton, and these remained dominant despite the influence of styles such as American Directoire and American Empire. Cabinetmakers like Phyffe adopted these styles before switching to the Greek revival.

Shaker furniture (1770–1800)

Shaker furniture is another unique and isolated pocket of design. The term originates from an English religious sect which went to America in 1774 and established itself in New England, Kentucky and Indiana. The simple harmony and utilitarian way of life of the Shakers is echoed in their furniture, whose whole beauty rests in the simplicity of the design. Shapes were kept as basic as possible and decoration, apart from simple turning, is nonexistent. The only concession toward embellishment was the use of stain to enhance the natural beauty of woods like maple, pine and fruitwood. Overall the Shaker style was way ahead of its time. Many modern designs are based upon it.

Below: A typical Shaker room from the American Museum in Britain.
Right: A mahogany Empire chest.
Below and bottom right: Two types of English Regency chairs. The saber-leg type dates from circa 1800.

Empire style (1800–15) and the second phase of neoclassicism (1800–25)

It is easy nowadays to view the neoclassical style as a massive series of plagiarisms from the ancient world of Rome, Greece and Egypt, but at the time designers and craftsmen really believed they were creating a new modern art. It fitted in to an overall philosophy – a way of viewing nature through the forms and sculptures of the ancient world. Where the first phase of neoclassicism is often tinged with a sentiment and a frivolous use of classical forms, Empire-style furniture has a more real and refreshing feel. As a development from the Directoire period a more academic approach was taken based on archaeological sources. The style eventually became universal and in England it is referred to as the Regency style after the prince Regent.

English Regency (1811–20)

These dates mark the period of the Regency in England but as a style the dates 1795–1825 are more accurate. It was really the last period of a readily identifiable style before the excesses and incoherencies of the Victorian era. Thomas Sheraton was largely responsible for forecasting and crystalizing this new style, and despite the various forms of classical, Egyptian, Gothic and Chinese, Regency furniture is simple and elegant. Except for chairs and some dining tables, nearly all Regency furniture was veneered. Surfaces were kept plain and decoration was limited to turning and brass inlay in grounds of rosewood and other exotic timbers. Other typical Regency features include ebony stringing, vertical reeding on the legs, simulated bamboo and painted decoration.

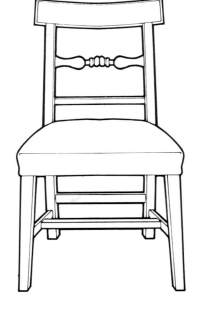

Right : An English Regency style sofa table. The top is veneered in rosewood, cross banded with satinwood.

American furniture (1810–40)

While the main centers of design in America were involved in the Federal, Directoire and Empire style, an important new branch of furniture was beginning to appear in the larger cabinet shops. This type was intended for a wider range of the population and took the form of a whole series of chairs and turned furniture. Two of the most common types were the Boston Rocker and the spool chair, usually made from all kinds of timbers and finished by painting and decorating. In this period fake graining and simulated-wood finishes started in a big way.

Early Victorian period (1840–1860)

The traditional methods of furniture construction persisted in many of the smaller cabinet shops throughout the early years of the nineteenth century but a host of new machine tools began to dominate furniture construction by about 1840. Power-driven planes, circular saws and rotary molding methods began to change furniture manufacturing from a craft into an industry.

Above: A Boston rocker, circa *1840.*

Although Victorian furniture is easy to recognize there is no particular and overall style that covers this extraordinary period. Many ideas were based on a host of retrogressive and romantic revivals. During the first half of the century many patterns from the past were copied, with the exception of those from the eighteenth century which the Victorians considered too recent a source and, strangely, a period of the dark ages of English Art. Popular furniture up to 1860 can be divided into four main styles. First, the influence of the Empire and Regency forms was still strong, so many pieces have a classical look with a strong bias toward Grecian forms. Second, the rococo style was revived in 1830, its main exponent in America being John Belter, who had developed the plywood technique for his elaborate furniture by about 1850. Third, in their search for a particularly English style that owed nothing to the continent, the Victorians unearthed the forms of Elizabethan and Jacobean furniture. Here they found another period in history which echoed their notion that Britannia ruled the waves and Englishmen's hearts were made of oak. Last, there is a mass of nameless furniture whose design is based around the Victorian's love of comfort and opulence.

Pieces from the early Victorian period are easy to spot, they are usually fairly small when compared with the monstrosities of the later period. Decoration, although fancy, is limited to carving; very few pieces are painted or made up from different or contrasting species of timber. On the whole it is extremely well made and has a plasticity that is lacking in the more rigid and crisper shapes that came after 1855.

Below: An ashwood ladder-back chair, circa 1888, designed by Ernest Gimson (1864–1919), a member of the English Arts and Crafts movement. This movement believed in sound design, constructional principles and a thorough understanding of materials.

Late Victorian period (1860–1900)

Furniture at this stage started to become massive and extremely elaborate. The general outline was more severe but heavy use was made of gilding, inlay carving, ormolu, painting and so forth. The making of furniture was no longer a craft but an industry run by people who had little idea about the technicalities of wood and cabinetmaking skills. The use of expensive cabinet woods such as mahogany, satinwood, rosewood and walnut was discontinued and by 1850 oak came back into fashion. Papier-mâché became common and many cheap woods were stained in imitation of more expensive woods. Oak was either used in the solid or veneered on a ground of plain oak. Cheap machine carving and the full use of labor-saving

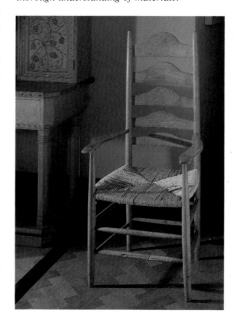

devices were the order of the day. These techniques dominated and although some attempt was made to return to simple and well-made furniture during the arts and crafts period of 1870–1914, the majority of popular furniture was made under these factory conditions.

Below: A French Art Nouveau style ashwood screen by Emile Galle, dated 1900.

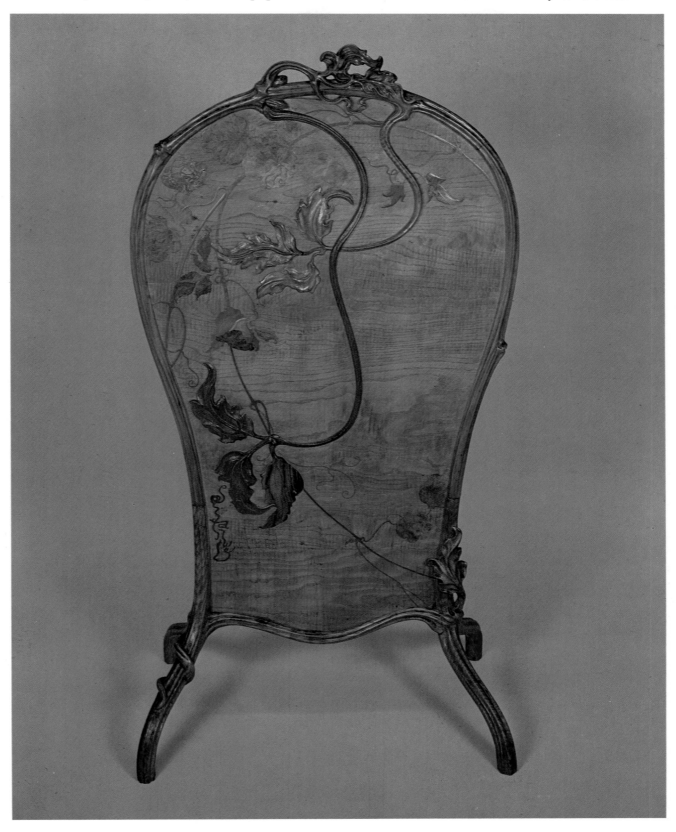

Edwardian period (1910–1920)

By about 1914 the popularity of oak was beginning to decline and furniture started to become smaller. As a reaction against the Victorian era of design the simpler forms of the Sheraton and Hepplewhite style were used to a large degree. Soft woods were used to a large extent and finished either with an antique stain or lacquer finish.

Modern furniture (1920–1980)

Apart from the art deco period of the 1920s and 1930s when avant-garde designers used tubular steel and molded laminates to enhance their use of rigid angles and curves, no modern style today can be considered universal. Comfort and simplicity seem to be the main criteria for mass-produced furniture; anything that is stylistically unique has usually come from the individual designer and craftsman.

Below: An Edwardian interior. Despite the obviously borrowed satinwood borders, stringing and narrow taper leg, all of the pieces in this room have a uniquely Edwardian flavor.

Right : A 1950s table. This type of leg (without its ears and stretchers) graces many a television set from the late 1950s, and 1960s.

Below right : A bentwood chair. Michael Thonet (1796–1871) began producing bentwood furniture as early as 1830. A staggering 50,000,000 copies of his simple cafe chair have been made since 1850.
Below far right : A standard mass-produced chair of the 1920s and 30s.

The reproduction

The above summary of furniture styles should start you off on the right track. Most of the types of early design are likely to be encountered in the form of the reproduction. Reproductions were first created in the Victorian period and have been made ever since.

Where the reproduction parts company with the fake is that the former usually exhibits only a token gesture toward simulating age. Paradoxically, although reproduction furniture is supposed to have an air of age about it, distressing and antiquing is kept to a minimum. This makes it sell better as although it is based on old designs it still looks shiny and new, which goes a long way to explain the staggering prices people pay for reproduction furniture. Often for a few dollars more it is possible to buy the real thing!

Most reproductions are made from cheap woods such as gum and whitewood and covered with a matching stain and polish to simulate expensive timbers like mahogany and cherry. It is not too hard to distinguish the modern reproduction from the antique; the grain is usually covered up and surfaces have a shine as opposed to a patina-

tion. Staining is often limited to the visible surfaces, leaving the underparts white and unfinished. On the better types the whole piece is stained but even here hidden parts have an artificial look about them, edges are sharp and surfaces appear uniform and clean. On an antique, even the wood which has not been exposed to handling and polishing has a look of age that is impossible to simulate with stain. It is hard to distinguish between the antique and the reproduction in pieces that were made at the turn of this century in styles like Hepplewhite, Sheraton, Louis XV and Louis XVI. These types were originally made from good-quality timber and after 60 years or so of careful wax polishing they often look more like an antique than the real thing.

Avoid using the reproduction as a guide to the various styles of furniture. Many designs are adapted to modern living and some really strange mutations occur, such as the Jacobean television cabinet, the Queen Anne rocker, the Chippendale cocktail table and the Empire telephone stand! On the same lines, straight reproduction copies are often incorrectly named; the Victorians with their cloudy and romantic view of history started this trend. Queen Anne-style chairs are usually labelled Chippendale.

Fakes and how to avoid them

This is a vast subject about which whole books have been written. Suffice it to say that if all the colonial artifacts were genuine the settlers must have been working 24 hours a day for our edification! In the early years of this century, faking was confined to the top end of the market as it was only worth faking the really expensive items. These days anything goes, particularly in the area of country furniture and the primitive types. Such furniture is valuable and as it is usually fairly simple it provides an ideal medium for the faker. A few pointers are listed below on how to view furniture and avoid the fake but in the main, with a bit of experience in restoration work and handling furniture you will soon learn to spot the spurious.

One/The altered piece. First, avoid the obvious. There is no such thing as a low antique coffee table or cocktail table – we will have to wait a few more decades before that comes on to the market. Such an object will be a reproduction, a Victorian marble-topped table that has had its legs shortened, or a gate leg table without its flaps and its base lowered. Large unfashionable lumps of furniture from the Victorian era usually go through a rebirth in the faker's hands. Often it is impossible to tell from the surface just what has happened. If you are suspicious in your first and overall impression of the piece, take a look inside to see whether the original construction lines show.

Two/Patination. Unless the faker uses old and ready-patinated timber, this is where he always slips up. Patination is quite simply the glass-like surface to wood and finishes achieved over the years by polishing and general use. The wood has a depth to it which is impossible to copy with speedy and chemical means. A quick trip to a museum will show you what this looks like.

Three/The quasi-antique and the made-from-old-wood story. These types of furniture incorporate one or two bits of genuine and decorative old wood into a totally new structure. The Victorians were past masters at this game so do not be distracted by the most obvious and decorative items. Make sure that everything matches and that the piece is not a marriage of two totally different pieces. Beware of the total fake made from bits of old floorboards and parts of beams from demolished houses. Oak is the usual medium as with age it goes dark

Facing page: A fine-quality reproduction chair, attributed to Hille of London, circa 1918. This firm began making ornate reproduction furniture in 1906 but by the 1950s they changed to designing furniture and are now one of the pioneers of modern design.

Below: The top picture shows a fake Jacobean joined stool made of old oak. The close-up shows the overdone signs of wear on the stretchers. Compare this to the genuine article in the center photograph. It is obvious that the faker has put his feet on the stretchers and then spokeshaved or chiselled the corresponding position out of the wood.

right to the core and so provides a ready base for faking stains. The total fake is the easiest to recognize as it usually has a tacky look to its surface. Sometimes the faker gets carried away and overdoes the signs of wear and tear – watch out for unnatural marks and bruising. Chains and pebbles – which are either hurled against the surface of the wood or hammered to leave a mark – are two of the faker's favorite distressing tools.

Four/Worm holes. Everyone knows what a 'guarantee' of age and authenticity worm holes provide! Ignore them completely as a means of authenticating a piece. In the right conditions the furniture beetle will infest any piece of furniture, modern or antique, in a matter of months. The only help that the worm provides is when the faker uses an old piece of wood which he has had to plane or cut to fit. While the larva of the beetle will eat its way in all directions under the surface of the timber, when it changes into the beetle it comes out through one neat hole. If you see all the channels exposed on the surface of a piece of wood you will know that someone has either planed the surface off or used a cut-down piece of wood from another piece of furniture.

Five/Materials and joints. Here again the practical experience of handling furniture is a tremendous help. A knowledge of the different types of timbers and when they were used is essential for the serious student. Good-quality timber should be hard and heavy, so if you find a piece that is incredibly light it will probably be reproduction. To come across an early nineteenth-century style chair which is made from the modern and pinky colored 'sapele' mahogany is an obvious anachronism so it is important to take note of when the various woods were used and how to recognize them. The thickness

Above: Gilt wood base to a chest. The joint has come open and shows twin dowels, indicating a date after 1840, although the style is Jacobean.

Below: A reconstructed William and Mary table. The top and drawers might be right but the legs and stretcher are replacements. Note how the piece has been distressed with a hammer.

of timber provides some interesting clues as well. Until recently hardwoods were relatively cheap so the craftsman could afford to pick and choose and be generous with his designs. The thickness of veneers provides some interesting pointers as to the age of a piece. Up until the end of the nineteenth century veneers were cut through the log for the better quality furniture in the plain-sawn fashion. This produced thicknesses of $\frac{1}{16}$ inch and more. Modern methods of placing the whole trunk of a tree on an enormous lathe and peeling off the veneer as you would unroll a scroll of paper produces sheets that are not as attractively marked and, for economy's sake, are paper thin. Plywood found in sheet form for cabinet tops and drawer bottoms is a sure indication of the twentieth century. Joints provide a useful guideline, twin dowelling was unheard of before the 1850s and as a general rule the more regular dovetailing is, the later it will be.

Six Tool marks. Modern machines leave a different set of marks to the old hand saws and planes. The circular saw was first used in about 1800 but it was not used on a large scale until the 1860s. As the blade rotates through the wood it leaves circular marks which are easy to spot; the frame and hand saw leave a series of parallel lines.

All the above tips cannot be used in isolation, they should be employed as a set formula for viewing furniture. To find circular-saw marks on the back boards of an eighteenth-century chest of drawers does not necessarily mean the piece is a fake. Above all, whether you intend to buy damaged furniture as an investment or simply for the experience of restoring it, it can be a great help if you ask yourself these questions: *One* Despite the damage, does the whole piece look original, whether it is antique, reproduction or modern? *Two* Are the woods and techniques used in keeping with the style and age of the piece? *Three* If modern, is it well made with sound wood joints as opposed to nails? *Four* Are the necessary tools, materials and woods available for its repair? *Five* Does it show signs of previous bad repairs and if so will they be easy to remedy?

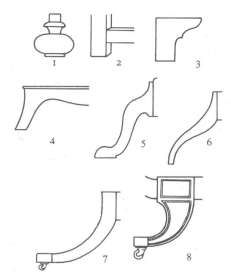

Above: 1–4, bun, stile and brackets.
5–7, 18th- and 19th-century tripods.
8, Grecian sofa scroll.

Below: 1, Bobbin. 2, Baluster. 3, Twist.
4, Cup and cover. 5, Flemish scroll
6, 'Square.' 7, Louis XV. 8, Plain cabriole.
9, Carved cabriole. 10, Taper.
11, Chippendale straight. 12, Hepplewhite
plain. 13, Hepplewhite decorated. 14, Adam.
15 and 16, Sabers. 17, Pre-Victorian.
18, American fancy. 19, Windsor.
20–23, Victorian. 24, Modern cabriole.

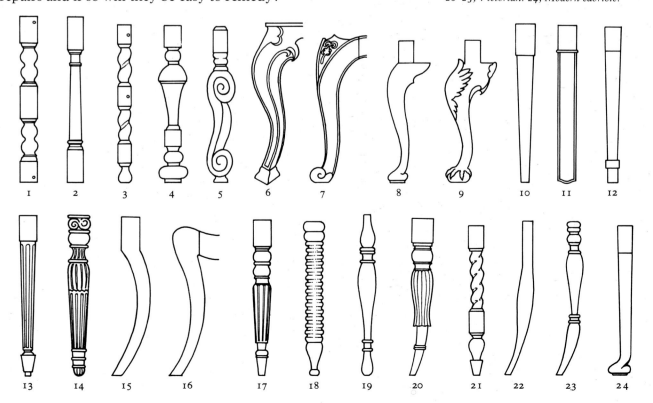

TOOLS and EQUIPMENT

One of the pleasures of furniture restoration is the variety of work to be found. No two jobs are ever exactly similar, consequently a fairly comprehensive tool collection is an advantage if you plan to restore on a full- or even part-time basis. When it comes to suggesting what sort of equipment to buy, those well worn maxims engendered by the wood-working crafts inevitably spring to mind – platitudes such as 'a bad workman always blames his tools' tells only half the story. Obviously, skilled restorers can effect considerable repairs with the simple kit of a craft knife, adhesive tape and glue but they will soon tell you that when it comes to buying hand tools, it always pays to purchase the best. In the long run a modest accumulation of well-maintained, good-quality equipment, coupled with some ingenuity and commonsense is a far better bet than a host of fancy and elaborate junk.

Naturally the choice of tools is governed by how much restoration work you intend to do. It must be somewhat disheartening for aspiring

Below: The restorer's workshop. Fiona Blaxill and Neil Batchelor at work, Workshop 8, Cirencester.
Fiona Blaxill is a natural, who dispels the belief that you have to be male and apprenticed to Chippendale to be a good restorer.

restorers to find themselves confronted with a massive list, so it is best to point out at this stage that not all the following suggestions are essential. You might find, for example, that the majority of clamping work can be done with a tourniquet and tape, without incurring the expense of buying a set of sash or pole clamps. Most households contain a basic tool kit, so if you simply intend to do running repairs to keep your furniture in order, you will probably have the basis for a collection already.

One way of forming a good collection is to buy secondhand equipment. It is usually half the price of new tools and, with a bit of experience, you can soon learn to spot the bargain hiding beneath a layer of grime and rust. Cleaning such tools with steel wool and oil will often reveal a steel far superior to the modern equivalent.

The workshop

Many surface repairs can be carried out in the home without a workshop. Missing veneer, dents, scratches and bruises can be seen to with the piece still *in situ*. Extensive structural repairs involving carpentry and the messy business of a large gluing job should be carried out in a garage or shed. A large floor area is preferable; apart from the fact that dismantled chairs and cabinets take up a lot of space, there is always a stage in restoration (usually the gluing process) when pieces have to be put to one side, so it is handy to have the room to carry on with something else.

Good natural daylight is essential for matching and staining new replacements. What might appear to be a perfect match under artificial light will stand out like a sore thumb in daylight. A few antique shops take advantage of this fact and usually have a gloomy section where even the least desirable and badly colored pieces will 'glow' appealingly! The workshop should also be fairly warm if you plan to do any polishing. Temperatures below 70 degrees Fahrenheit can cause all kinds of problems with the chemicals used in restoration. A fan heater is useful in a very cold environment since it can be directed at dismantled furniture until the joints are warm to the touch, a necessity if you use the old-type cabinetmaker's glue.

A sturdy workbench should be your next concern. This should be about 3 feet long, 2 feet wide and 2 feet 9 inches high with a good-quality wood-working vise bolted through the top and positioned at one end. If you are short of space the versatile Black & Decker Workmate is ideal as it can be folded down and hung on the wall when not in use.

Hand tools

Clamps and Holding Devices Most adhesives need to have pressure applied during the setting process, so clamps are essential for squeezing the excess glue out of the joint and forming a good wood-to-wood contact. The cheapest and simplest of these devices is the Spanish windlass or tourniquet clamp made by passing a loop of cord around the object and then tightening it up by twisting a rod in the cord. A selection of C-clamps and hand screws are recommended for work that is too large to be held by tape. The wide-throat variety will reach quite a distance into table tops for holding inlaid repairs. Repairing parts of furniture that are round in section requires the use of hose clamps or jubilee clips. They provide an all-round even pressure where a C-clamp would slip off the curved surface. Along with adhesive tape and spring clips, a selection of heavy-duty rubber bands and clothes pegs are useful for holding awkward shapes such

as applied moldings and carvings.

For cabinet and chair repairs where a multitude of joints require gluing at the same time, it is really a matter of personal preference whether you choose the pipe or sash, webbing, wire or frame clamp. All are good for tightening up joints and for general carcass repairs.

Locking jaw pliers complete the picture in the clamping department. They pay for themselves over and over when it comes to holding edge veneer as well as for removing those obstinate rusty screws whose heads have broken off.

Saws There are three essential saws for wood – the panel, tenon or backsaw, and the coping saw. The first can be used for cutting timber down to size while the tenon saw is a must for cutting accurate joints and for general benchwork. When buying this second type make sure that the steel or brass back is heavy and stout so that the weight of the saw will cut without you having to force it at all. Both the coping saw and its cousin the fret saw can be used for shaped work, for marquetry repairs and for cutting thick veneer. For really fine joinery a good-quality dovetail saw has to be recommended. Quite often in restoration a small but fairly long saw is needed for reaching into inaccessible places so the pad or keyhole saw is an inexpensive but useful item.

You will be surprised how often you will have to resort to a metal-cutting saw. Sometimes someone will have hammered nails into a piece in a cheap and often useless attempt to hold it together. The hacksaw and the mini hacksaw will cope with these hidden bits of metal as well as proving indispensable for cutting metal fittings such as handles and locks.

Boring Tools and Associated Equipment The power drill is extremely useful in the workshop, although for furniture repairs the hand wheel brace and the brace plus a selection of bits are more accurate for drilling out sockets for pegs and dowels. One useful attachment for the brace is the screwdriver bit which gives tremendous torque for removing rusted screws. A general-purpose cabinet screwdriver plus an electricians screwdriver will cope with both small and large screws. You might like to add to this selection a center punch with a hollow point and a hand bradawl for making starting holes for screws and for testing for the presence of nails in timber.

Hammers and Chisels A small wooden mallet with a 4-inch head is all you will need for knocking furniture apart and for driving your chisels. Alternatively the new rubber and vinyl faced mallets can be used for much the same purpose, they are designed not to bruise wood. Two other types are useful: a carpenters claw hammer for removing and driving nails and finally a small ball pien hammer for more delicate work.

A selection of fine chisels ranging in size from $\frac{1}{8}$ of an inch to 1 inch are needed for dealing with the carpentry side of restoration. These should be ground at a fairly shallow angle – about 20 degrees – and finished off on the oil stone at the same angle. This gives you a razor-sharp edge that will cut with hand pressure alone, even through the toughest and oldest timbers. Do not worry at first about a set of carving chisels, they are of course useful but initially much shaped and carved work can be carried out with a coping saw, wood files, sandpaper and a craft knife.

Planes, Shapers, Files and Knives Furniture restoration requires a good-quality block plane coupled with a jack plane for long surface areas that require a dead-true line for gluing. Considering that much repair work is fairly small in area size, one of the most useful planes is

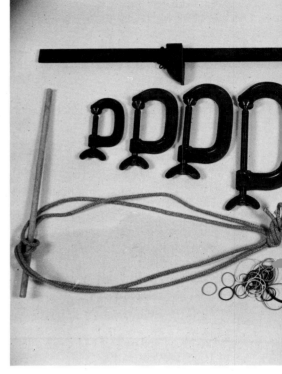

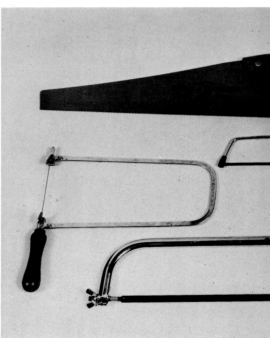

Top: Clamps. First row: Sash or pole clamp. Second row: Various C-Clamps; picture frame clamp. Third row: windlass, hose clamps, web strap. Bottom row: elastic bands, clothes pegs, locking-jaw pliers.
Above: Saws. Top row: combined saw, dovetail saw. Second row: mini-hacksaw, key-hole saw. Third row: fret saw, tenon saw. Bottom row: hacksaw, coping saw.

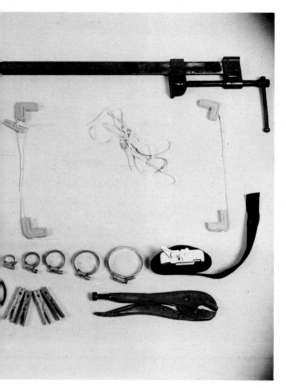

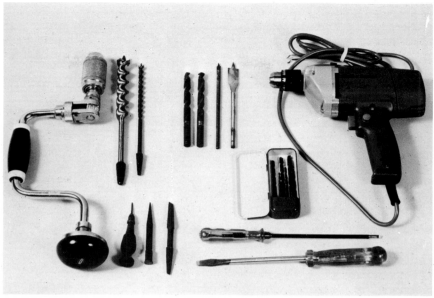

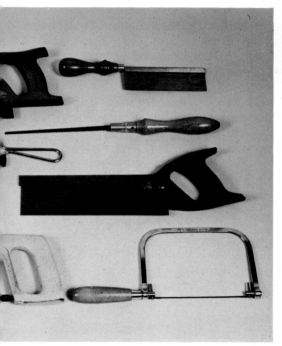

Top: Boring tools. Top row: Swing brace and 2 bits, 4 high-speed bits, electric drill and box of bits. Bottom row: Bradawl, center punch, screwdriver bit, electrician's screwdriver, cabinet screwdrivers.

Above: Hammers and chisels. Left to right: Carving chisels, wood chisels, mallet, ball pien hammer and claw hammer. Bottom: Vinyl and rubber-faced mallet.

the shoulder or bull nose plane. Here the cutting blade goes right across the sole of the plane, thus enabling it to be used right up against right angles and in small corners. Make sure that the detachable nose of this plane is half the length of that of the back piece so that there is a good face area for accurate planing.

Many professional restorers have a collection of old beechwood molding planes. They can still be picked up at sales and auctions, usually in sets of 10 or 20 and at a fairly good price. Though rarely used they are a joy to handle when large amounts of heavy moldings are missing from antique furniture.

For round and curved work a spokeshave and two or three surform tools are handy. They are particularly good for roughing out and for rapidly reducing large areas of timber. In addition, an assortment of three-square, rat-rail, half-round and flat files should be acquired for both metal and wood repairs.

Two of the most useful tools in restoration are the cabinet scraper and the marking and cutting knife. For really fine work such as slitting blistered veneer in order to get new glue under the surface, the surgeons scalpel is highly recommended. Their blades are so fine and sharp that they rarely bruise the wood and once the veneer is relaid the cut line is invisible. Several strokes are needed when cutting thick veneer with a scalpel otherwise the flexible blade will snap and fly off. Protective goggles should be worn!

Marking, Measuring and Testing Tools Measuring work in cabinet repairs must be accurate, particularly in pieces of a later date where most of the components will have been made by machine. On antique pieces this criteria does not always apply since an allowance has to be made for the nature of handmade components. If you examine a seventeenth-century table with turned legs, all the legs, though basically of the same design, will differ slightly. The pattern was usually repeated by eye and with the help of a crude template. Most professional restorers will trust their eyes rather than a rule to judge how a replacement looks in relation to the rest of the piece. It is always a good idea to cut new work slightly oversize when making carpentry repairs. It can always be trimmed later to conform with any idiosyncrasies caused by shrinkage and warping, but if cut too small, nothing can be done.

Repaired joints should always be a tight fit, so for this sort of work the try square, sliding bevel and mortise gauge save a lot of time in producing the correct lines for cutting. Use the remaining parts of the piece of furniture that are still intact as a pattern for replacements, you should be able to get your measurements with either the mortise gauge or a pair of calipers. If you cannot work with the comparison method of making replacements, then the folding carpenter's rule is essential. A metal ruler is handy for measuring and acting as a guide for cutting with the craft knife. The contour gauge is useful when whole sections of moldings have to be replaced and for copying turned legs and so forth by hand.

Miscellaneous Tools These tools, although infrequently used, can be a great help. Top of the list is a pair of pliers for removing nails and for straightening bent metalwork. For those stubborn screws and metal repairs a soldering iron is useful. Applied to the head of a screw, It causes the metal to expand in the wood. Once cool, the screw can be extracted quite easily. A small gas-operated blow torch is useful. Directed over a joint coated with old cabinetmaker's glue, the flame will cause the adhesive to become toffee-like and then turn to powder. Once the powder is brushed off the joint will be dry and clean. A wire brush, tooth brush and one or two old chisels should dispense with the more modern and tougher adhesives to be found in joints.

Where a joint is stuck fast but needs to be released in order to effect a proper repair, a hypodermic syringe is extremely effective. This should be of the type that can be boiled in water so that it can also be used for injecting hot beeswax and chemical resins into worm-eaten wood as well as for pumping the appropriate solvent down a glue line. If you can get your hands on an old smoothing iron, it will save a lot of time when re-laying blistered veneer.

Top: Planes and forming tools.
Clockwise: Spokeshave, three old molding planes, smoothing plane, jack plane, two surforms, bull-nose or shoulder plane, Stanley knife, scalpel, cabinet scraper, and files.
Above: Measuring and marking tools.
Top row: Try square, tape measure, folding carpenter's rule. Bottom row: Profile gauge, ruler, compasses, calipers, sliding bevel, mortise gauge.

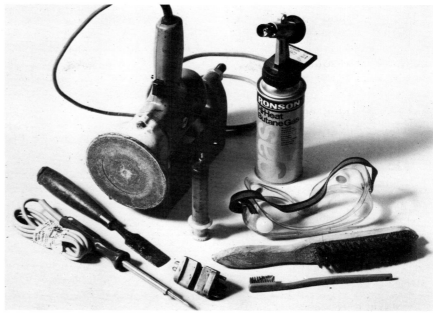

Homemade tools

A great deal of time and money can be saved by making a few devices. As with any tool, their usefulness depends on the inventiveness of the user.

Folding Wedges This is a cheap and effective method of clamping two boards together. An elongated H shape is made in 2×3-inch timber, as illustrated. When the two wedges are driven together with hammers, pressure is applied to the meeting surfaces of the join. Several of these can be made up to cope with different sized boards.

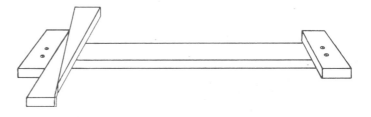

Softening blocks Furniture is easily damaged during the restoration process, particularly softwoods and polished surfaces. To avoid this, various lengths of scrap timber should be covered in thick cloth (this can be stapled and glued on) so that when a piece is turned upside down it can be kept clear of the workshop floor. Use pieces of wood to act as packing between metal clamps and finished surfaces.

Shooting board This is a device used mainly by the cabinetmaker but it can be employed for table-top boards whose edges have warped and consequently are impossible to glue. Minor discrepancies in the meeting surfaces can be planed out by eye but when the edges are really bad the shooting board produces a surface that is flat and true to the right angle. Two 4-foot lengths of perfectly planed and ready-cut timber should be purchased from the wood merchant. The first (board A) should be 9 inches $\times$ 1 inch. The second and narrower length (board B) which measures 6 inches $\times$ 1 inch is glued and screwed to the top of A so that a 3-inch rabbet is formed. Three 9-inch lengths of 2×1 are then secured to the underside of A and a further $6 \times 2 \times 1$ inch strip made fast to the top and end of B to act as

Top right: Clockwise: Soldering iron, old chisel, rigid sanding disk, syringe, blowtorch, goggles, wire brush, toothbrush, and honing guide.
Above right: A homemade folding wedge.

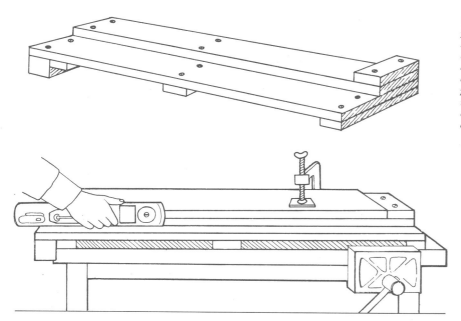

Left: A shooting board. It is essential to use a plane with a long sole such as the medium-size smoothing or jack type. This avoids making dips in the edge of the board. The minimum amount of wood should be removed from the edges of planks or old plank tables, particularly if the table is circular. If too much is taken off, a series of 'steps' will show on the edge of the table top when the circular top is reglued.

a stop. To prevent the device from slipping on the workbench, a 2-inch timber square should be applied under board A at the opposite end to the stop. The wood to be planed is placed on the upper part of board B so that its end rests against the stop. A jack or similar parallel-sided plane is laid on its side and pushed up and down with the right hand. The work can either be clamped or held by hand so that when the plane is pressed against the face of A, it acts as a guide and produces a straight and right-angled edge on the work. Once both edges of, for example, an offending table top, are planed in this manner they should fit perfectly and provide a good gluing surface.

Scratch stock Anyone who has ever tried to make a length of replacement molding will tell you what a laborious process it is without the use of the proper implement. So great is the variety of moldings to be found in both old and new furniture that frequently the home-made scratch stock is the only way of avoiding the time-consuming process of carving by hand. This indispensable little tool has been used since the seventeenth century for making small moldings. It simply consists of a block of wood (with a notch cut out of it) cut in two and then screwed together again so that the two parts may be loosened at will and any variety of cutters inserted. The cutters can be made from bits of flat steel sawn off an old cabinet scraper with the hacksaw. Using a variety of files, the cutter is shaped to the reverse of the molding. The blade is inserted into the block and then the whole is drawn across the wood with the edge pressed hard up against the notch. You will be surprised how accurate this tool is even on the toughest and most brittle of timbers. If you have whole sections of moldings missing it is worth spending the half hour or so required to file the cutter to shape. The only disadvantage of this tool is that it cannot cope with moldings wider than 1 inch; the blade tends to vibrate as it is drawn across the wood, producing a wave-like pattern in the surface. All types of blades can be made for the stock, including one that will make the grave for inlaying stringing.

Stringing planer Many types of stringings can be purchased from wood stockists, though not all of them will fit into the grave, particularly on handmade furniture. A useful tool can be made for planing stringing down to size with a block of hardwood, a small C-clamp and a Stanley Knife blade. The block should measure

Below: The scratch stock. It is helpful to make the molding on the edge of a large piece of wood, which can be gripped firmly in a vise. This can be cut to the required depth afterward. Short lengths of molding can be made without fixing the cutter into the stock, the blade being held in the fingers like a cabinet scraper. See page 113.

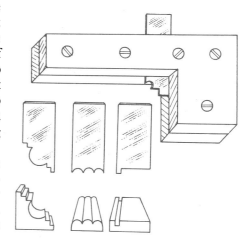

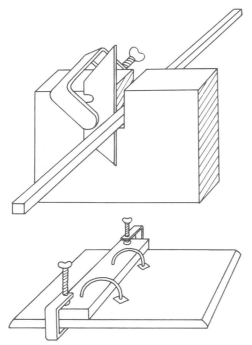

roughly 4 inches square by 1 inch thick. A ¼-inch × 1 inch dado is cut into the center of the block and then the Stanley blade is clamped on so that it protrudes parallel and slightly over the dado. The piece of stringing is fed in from the back and then pulled through and in the process is reduced in width by the blade. By continually turning the piece of stringing over after each pull, a smooth and perfect square is maintained. Repeated adjustment to the blade will ensure a gradual reduction in size.

Veneer patch holder This useful homemade device will enable you to apply pressure to patches of veneer that are right in the middle of large table tops and therefore out of reach of the C-clamp. Metal spring clips or flexible steel wire from upholstery springs can be bent to shape and then fixed into a length of timber so that they hang below the surface of the wood. Once the timber is clamped at either end to the table top the wire will apply pressure to the patches. A rigid piece of transparent plastic should be placed between the wire and the wood. This will distribute the pressure over the patch and allow you to see whether the wood is bedding down correctly in its grave.

Power tools

Power tools and attachments Any motorized tool is a wise investment for someone who plans to do a lot of restoration work which requires extensive ground work and carpentry repairs. Such machines as routers, saber and circular saws and sanders dispense with the time-consuming task of shaping and cutting wood by hand. However, the majority of tasks, particularly in the finishing stages, can be carried out with hand tools. In fact the latter often produce a repair far more in keeping with the older types of furniture. Antiques rarely appear as a series of immaculate level surfaces, straight lines and perfect curves that the machine tools produce. Most of the tools recommended in this section are only used for the background repairs – carpentry work as opposed to restoration.

A power drill is an asset and should, if possible, be fitted with an accelerator trigger so that a whole range of speeds is available. An essential attachment for the drill is a bench stand and rigid circular sander. With the drill inverted and fixed rigidly by its horizontal stand to the workbench, the circular sander can be used for producing straight edges on bits of wood that have to be dropped into recesses

Top: Stringing planer. It is essential to use a new, heavy-duty Stanley knife blade when using this tool. An old, but sharp, plane blade can be used in place of the Stanley. (Clamp it so that the bevel faces away from the block.) The base of the block is clamped into the vise to provide purchase for pulling the stringing through.

Above: A veneer patch holder. Use a drill bit slightly smaller than the diameter of the wire to make the holes in the wood. One end of the circle can then be forced into these while the other hangs at least two inches below the wood. This will apply local pressure to the veneer patch. Place something between the wood and the wire, otherwise the end of the spring will go clean through the veneer.

Right: Using the rigid circular sander. When sanding small pieces of wood it is very important to use a medium-grade abrasive paper, and to first take the 'bite' out of the paper with a piece of pine. If you do not do this, the grit will lock into the wood, fling it across the workshop and may injure you. Sanders can be purchased as an integral unit complete with tilting table.

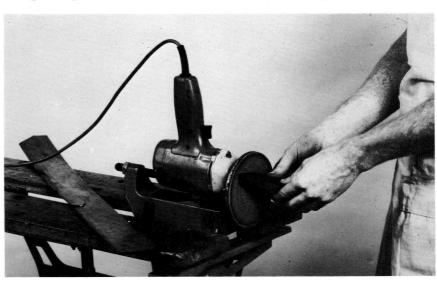

or butted up against the work where sections are missing. The sander is particularly useful when repairs to antique veneer are needed, since you can sand the back off an old bit of wood to get it to the right thickness without affecting the existing and ready-patinated surface. This way, staining is unnecessary if your wood is the same color and age as the piece being repaired. Once you have gone to the expense of buying a horizontal drill stand you have a versatile tool into which other useful accessories such as grinding, buffing wheels and polishing heads can be fixed.

A circular saw can either be in the form of an attachment to your drill or a separate unit on its own. It does not have to have a massive blade, a 5-inch diameter will do to start with. This will give you a cutting edge of up to $1\frac{3}{8}$ inches. For timber over $1\frac{3}{8}$ inches thick, reverse the wood and cut from the other side so that the kerf lines meet and thus produce a cut of $2\frac{3}{4}$ inches. Furniture repairs usually involve taking the replacement wood to the power machine as opposed to the other way round, so a saw table is always a bonus. Here the circular saw is reversed and clipped up into the saw table so that veneer sheets can be cut off a block of timber and wood can be cut to exactly the right thickness. Such a table will provide a great deal more control over your work as you can see how the cut is progressing, whereas when using the saw by hand it is not always possible to gauge what is going on beneath the sole plate of the saw.

To qualify as the 'complete' restorer a làthe is required. It is usually a fairly expensive item but indispensable when a large amount of restoration is undertaken. Bun feet, drawer knobs, turned legs, spindles and so on can be copied and replaced easily with a lathe. A set of wood-turning chisels has to be used: it would be very dangerous to use ordinary chisels which would snap under such high pressure.

Top: Squaring up the edges of a cabinet scraper with a file, prior to smoothing on the oil stone.
Above: Turning back the edge of the scraper. Turn back both sides to produce a minute 'T' shape on the scraper edge.

Left: Working with small pieces of wood is peculiar to restoration. It is often helpful to take the wood to the tool. When used in this fashion plane blades have to be extremely keen and finely set, so that the wood almost powders off.

Above: Using the scraper. Thumb pressure produces a slight bend in the steel, which lifts the sharp corners off the wood. With experience, you can level a replacement patch of veneer or thicker wood without touching or marking the surrounding surface.

Bottom: Turning back the edge of a plane blade after honing.
Below: Good woodwork, cabinetmaking and restoration depend on sharp tools. Generally speaking, the older a piece of wood gets, the harder it is. It helps to continually maintain the edge on your chisels. The honing guide illustrated should be used in a figure eight pattern so that the stone is worn evenly.

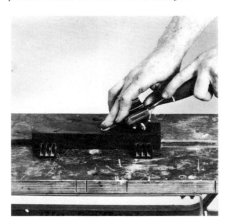

A **cabinet scraper** is useful too. It is designed to give a better finish to a piece of wood that is already worked or machined. The woodworking variety consists of a rectangular strip of steel measuring about $\frac{1}{16} \times 6 \times 3$ inches. For finer work, like removing or flattening out a polished surface prior to the final coat, the steel strip is even thinner. To sharpen the scraper, set the steel strip in the vise and run a fine file flat over the protruding edge. Remove the burr by rubbing a fine oil stone on the top and the sides so that the edges are really sharp and square. To produce the cutting part, turn back the edges with the aid of a hard round steel object (for example the back of a gouge chisel) held at an angle of 45 degrees. The sharpened edge is thus transformed into a smooth and razor-like burr which acts as the scraping edge.

To use the scraper, hold the blade in both hands so that it slants away from you, at a slight angle to the perpendicular. A small bend is produced by placing the thumbs in the center of the scraper while your fingers grip the side away from the body. Place the lower edge on the work and push the whole edge away from the body. At the end of each stroke lift the scraper off the surface in the same gradual movement to avoid making stop lines in the wood.

It takes quite some time to master this tool but it is worth the effort. Usually the scraper is used in the same direction as the grain, though sometimes the wood will fur up and have to be worked from a different direction. Here, experience is the only guide.

Workshop maintenance

To ensure a long life and years of use from your tools, a little care and maintenance is essential. A good workshop should be well-planned so that everything is within easy reach and has its allotted place. Tools that are left lying around or stacked away in a haphazard fashion will inevitably get their working edges chipped or broken. It is usual to fix wooden racks and boards to the walls around the workbench so that chisels and the like are kept free from marring surfaces and can be put away after each job. The workbench and floor area often become congested, particularly during the lengthy restoration processes. It is often a good idea to have a box fitted with felt-lined racks that can be trailed around the workshop and used as a receptacle for tools which are constantly needed. You have to work round large pieces like a chest of drawers which are too big to go on the workbench; you can take the tools with you.

Even with constant use tools are prone to rust attack, and it can spread like wildfire. After use, metal surfaces should be wiped over with an oil-soaked rag to prevent any deterioration. Chemicals, dyes and stains should have their own separate unit if possible, such as an old doorless cupboard, which should be placed in a different section of the workshop, away from the tools. Acids, alkalies and bleaches, if not corked properly, can attack nearby metal surfaces

Of all the cutting tools, chisels require the most maintenance since they are in constant use. If they are ground back at a shallow angle and without a bevel they will cut through even the hardest timbers. Unfortunately, a 20-degree edge means that they will damage very easily if you hit an old nail, so it is always best to test the timber first. Constant honing on the oil stone will avoid a rounded edge. Continual sharpening by hand also reduces the likelihood of having to regrind the blade. To achieve a really flat and true angle by hand takes quite a bit of practice so a honing guide is useful. This is simply a clamp with a running wheel underneath into which the chisel can be

fixed. Smear a few drops of oil on the stone and roll the blade back and forward in a figure-eight movement so that the stone is worn evenly. Once the edge is sharp remove the chisel from the guide and reverse on the stone so that the burr can be turned back. Finally, to achieve that razor-sharp edge, use an oil-soaked leather strop (an old leather belt, for example).

Above: By clamping a piece of timber level with the oil stone, it is easy to get a good edge on a wide-blade plane with the honing guide. With practice, the honing guide becomes redundant and edges can be sharpened by hand.

Adhesives

The strength and life of any glue depends ultimately on how it is used and whether the correct type is used for the job. Initially, gluing appears to be a simple process, but unless carried out properly and in accordance with the instructions, failure, even partial failure, can be disastrous. The collapse of just one joint in a reglued chair or cabinet usually means that the job has to be restarted from scratch. To avoid such occurrences follow three basic rules.

Choice of glue Most glues work best with one material. Wood adhesives are designed to penetrate into the porous surfaces of timber, in theory producing thousands of little teeth that help to lock the glue to the surface. The multipurpose epoxy-resin glues seem the ideal choice for the workshop, as they work on a variety of materials but they only play a small part in furniture restoration. Being thick and resinous in nature, they lack penetrating qualities and are best suited for smooth and nonporous surfaces like glass, china and metal. Glue for rejointing furniture should be special wood glues, chosen on whether it is best suited for outdoor, modern interior or antique furniture. Outdoor furniture needs a waterproof glue, such as the urea-formaldehyde variety. Indoor furniture can be repaired with polyvinyl glue, though most restorers tend to use the same water-soluble adhesive used in the repair of antique furniture. They consider it foolhardy to use glue which cannot be reactivated once cured. Once glued, future repairs become exceedingly difficult and time consuming. There is always a chance that the furniture will be misused or the components broken, and soluble glue then proves a blessing. On antique furniture old cabinet glue is really the only type that should be used. Occasionally, where clamping is impossible, a contact cement has to be used. These rubber-based glues are also used to re-lay veneer on modern pieces.

Clean surfaces All areas to be bonded should be clean, dry and free from grease. This is essential for ensuring a good fixing. New glue rarely sticks to old, so existing meeting faces should be cleaned to ensure good wood-to-wood contact. The one exception is hide glue, but even here it is best to remove the residue.

Method of application Manufacturers instructions must be followed carefully. All meeting surfaces should be thoroughly covered in glue but the less there is in the final joint the better. A good fixing relies on close contact between the surfaces, not on the glue itself. Whenever possible, clamps and holding devices should be used to squeeze out the excess glue and to maintain a constant pressure until the adhesive has cured completely. Finally, a warm workshop will speed the drying time of most glues.

Glues derived from organic substances

One/Animal glue is first and foremost a type of glue for furniture restoration. Prior to the 1930s it was the main adhesive for furniture making and consequently it is in keeping to use it to repair such pieces. This glue has an amazing ability to amalgamate with itself. Even if it is impossible to clean awkward joints thoroughly the new glue will mix and adhere to the old.

It consists of a gelatine made from boiling down hoofs, skins and horns, and once dry is sold as a powder/flake, slab or pearl. Place the glue in a jam jar, just cover in water, and leave for 24 hours. Once it has turned to jelly place the jar in an old pan full of water and heat up until it is like thin cream. (Put a thin piece of wood between the pan and the glass to avoid cracking the glass.) If the glue is too thick, add more water until it runs off the brush in a thin unbroken line. It is important not to boil the glue, nor to keep on reheating it, as both weaken the glue. Make up slightly more than required and start afresh with a new batch for each job.

Although this glue cures in 24 hours, it sets initially in about 5 minutes so it is important to have all clamps and softening blocks ready for immediate application. Being a hot glue, it is imperative that all meeting surfaces are warmed before it is applied. Cold joints chill the glue and make it rubbery. Where clamps are impractical, butt joints can be rubbed back and forth until the glue sets. When holding devices are used, they should be left on overnight.

Most small workshops do not bother with this glue because of the lengthy preparation but when a lot of restoration is undertaken it is indispensable. Once you have accustomed yourself to the somewhat objectionable smell and have mastered its use, you will use no other. Types and names: Hide, cabinet, scotch, pearl

Two/Like cabinet glue, this adhesive has been used for centuries. An early type, used in the seventeenth century, was made from cheese. Casein itself forms the base for many types of paint used on antique furniture, normally called milk paint. The glue consists of skimmed milk and a mild acid and comes as a white powder. Used cold and mixed with water it is extremely strong and more water resistant than cabinet glue. Unfortunately some types stain some hardwoods and cannot be used for rubbed joints as the glue itself is not sticky. Clamps are needed at all times. It is useful to the restorer as a binder for powdered colors. Types: Casco, Certus, Croid Insol

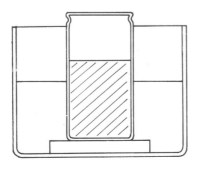

Below: A homemade pot for dissolving and heating cabinet glue. The water level should be below that of the glue, and a piece of wood placed under the jar to avoid cracking the glass.

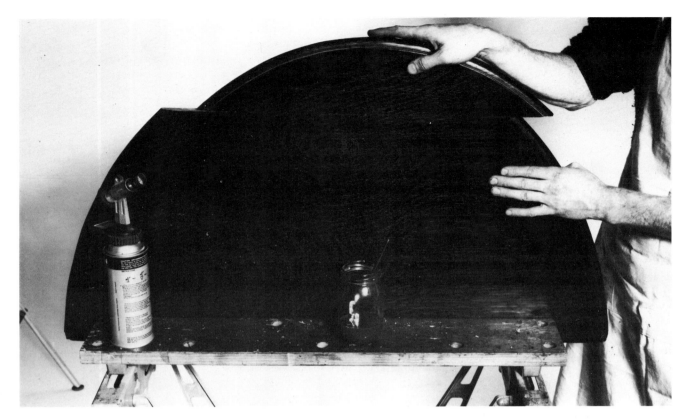

Celluloid cement Developments in the early part of this century produced the celluloid-based glues, manufactured by dissolving celluloid in acetone or amyl acetate. These are considered to be the first multipurpose household glues. They are characterized by their pungent smell and by the fact that they become transparent when dry. Celluloid glue comes in a tube and can be used as an undercoat for gluing metal inlays with epoxy resin. Types: Duco cement, Durofix, Evostick clear.

Resin-based adhesives The many varieties of this glue were developed by chemists in the 1930s for wartime use. They are of the cold-setting type and are consequently easier to handle than the traditional animal glues. For reference they can be divided into two categories: those that are not waterproof and are suitable for indoor furniture, and those that are water-resistant.

One/Polyvinyl acetate (PVA) is a cold-setting resin glue used by many woodworkers for indoor furniture. It is extremely strong and the thick white liquid can be used straight from the container. It works best when clamped but can also be used for rubbed joints. Oak and other woods with a high tannic acid content will sometimes darken this glue. Similar types include the Aliphatic polymer varieties that have a faster setting time. Types: Elmer's wood glue, Borden's, Bostick carpentry, Evostick Resin W, Unibond, Dufix, Dunlop woodworking, Casco PVA, Croid, Timbabond.

Two/Urea and Resorcinol resin glues. Synthetic-resin adhesives come in several forms, either as the glue and hardener already mixed and activated by water, or as a resinous syrup which precipitates the reaction when mixed with the powder glue. These glues have the advantages of being waterproof, having a long shelf life and gap-filling qualities. Mixed with the appropriate type of sawdust they make an admirable filler or stopping. Types: Cascamite.

Three/Epoxy-resin. The two-part Epoxy-resin adhesives have

Above: The rubbed joint. By thoroughly cleaning the edges of the board it is possible to make a strong joint with cabinet glue by simply rubbing the joint until it 'locks.' It is essential to warm the meeting faces and make sure that they join perfectly before applying the glue. The blow torch should be run in a series of rapid passes from the unfinished side of the board so that it warms slowly and the polish is unaffected. The top should be left in the vertical position for 24 hours.

only a small place in furniture restoration. Thin and less-resinous types can be purchased from toy shops for wood gluing but even these are only suited for repairing badly wormed wood where it is necessary to conserve as much of the original as possible. Sponge-like wood which has to be veneered over can be solidified with this glue. However it is only used as a last resort. Its main use is for metal inlay. Types: Araldite, Borden Superfast.

Contact and impact cements Latex- and acrylic-based glues are useful when clamping is impractical or when other types of materials have to be bonded to wood, such as fabric or leather. The adhesive is coated on both surfaces, left to dry and then brought together so that the bond is immediate. Once bonded, separation or further repositioning is extremely difficult so accuracy has to be the order of the day. Types: Elmers, 3M Fastbond, Weldwood, Evostick Impact, Bostic 3.

Cyanoacrylate monomer adhesive A modern development. The so-called super glues have one main place in the field of restoration – to repair the groundwork on late eighteenth- and nineteenth-century mirror or picture frames. Many of these articles are composed of elaborate shapes cast around a wire core with a hardened gesso called compo. When such delicate parts get broken or crack badly it is impossible to clamp them without causing further damage. Super glue, being a very thin liquid, will penetrate into the smallest crack and you can hold the two parts in the fingers until it sets (about 5 seconds). Several shots are sometimes needed into the crack because of the absorbent nature of gesso. It is a fast and effective method but needs to be handled carefully as this glue will bond your fingers together. Super glues can also glue marble together.

Materials

Most of the materials used in restoration will be referred to in greater detail in later chapters. The following brief summaries are intended to provide a reference for the basic abrasives, chemicals, stains and so forth. The majority of these can be bought, when the need arises, from chemists, hardware stores and wood-supply firms.

Abrasives

Papers Abrasive papers are used mainly for shaping and sanding replacement parts and for general carpentry repairs. Coarse grades of garnet, aluminium oxide and silicon carbide are best suited for heavy-duty work such as that required of the rigid circular sander. They have a long life and do not clog easily. Medium grades of glass, garnet and silicon will remove fair amounts of wood without leaving heavy score lines on the surface. Fine glass and silicon carbide should be used for smoothing between coats of varnish prior to the final top coat. Silicon carbide, referred to as 'wet-and-dry,' can be lubricated with water or the appropriate thinner for that superfine finish.

Steel wool For stripping finishes, restorers prefer to use steel wool as it provides more control when removing heavy paint and dirty varnishes. Even under the thickest layers there rests a thin casing around the wood which will act as the base for rebuilding the patina. The overenthusiastic use of abrasive paper will cut through and destroy this casing so that it becomes extremely difficult to build up a shine. The exposed pores of the wood have to be refilled and the grain closed up again; a process that is never as satisfactory as conserving the original surface. Grades 0, 00, 000 of steel wool are the most commonly used types.

Powders Household cleaning agents which come in powder form work remarkably well in cleaning dirty and grubby furniture. The finest types, designed not to scratch the enamel of baths, can be made into a thin paste with water, wiped over the surface and cleaned off immediately with a dry cloth. These fine abrasive cleaners work well even on shellac and French-polished surfaces providing you do not use too much water. Too much water can cause the polish to bloom and go white. The finer grades of pumice powder and rottenstone can be used with water or the appropriate thinner for the final sanding action on polishes or for dulling overshiny surfaces.

Chemicals and allied substances used in restoration

Bleaches and acids Oxalic acid and proprietary AB bleach solution remove marks from surfaces and lighten replacements to match.

Alkalies All alkalies react with the natural acids in most hardwoods to produce toning and darkening effects. They include ammonia, bichromate of potash, household soda, American potash, slaked lime.

Stains and dyes Spirit stains are composed of aniline dye powder dissolved in methylated spirits or alcohol with French polish as a binder. Colors are Bismarck brown, mahogany, green, orange, oak, walnut, yellow, black and purple. Oil stain is a loose term covering the proprietary stains that can be thinned with turps substitute, for instance Jacobean oak, mahogany, walnut and so on. Homemade types can be made by dissolving oil-soluble aniline dyes in turpentine with gold size as the binder. Colors are as above and types include asphaltum dissolved by gentle heating in turpentine and creosote. Water stains are aniline dyes which are soluble in water. Varieties include Vandyke brown crystals dissolved in ammonia and water to make oak and walnut stain, mahogany powder stain, eosin powder, and animal or casein glue is added as binder.

Pigments Powder colors miscible in water or oil with the appropriate binding agent for painted surfaces, and milk paint. Colors are brown umber, burnt sienna, raw sienna, yellow ocher, flake white, lamp black, burnt umber.

Oils Three-in-one lubricant, best American turpentine, raw and boiled linseed oil, turps substitute (white spirit), white polishing or mineral oil, and Kerosene are all used.

Waxes Beeswax, paraffin and carnauba are used for making wax polishes, fillers, stopping and homemade furniture waxes.

Spirits Methylated spirits (denatured alcohol) benzene and gasoline are necessary.

Varnishes, lacquers and polishes

One/Gold size is used for laying gold leaf and as the binder for colors ground in oil.

Two/Shellac flakes. Best quality pale orange. Soluble in methylated spirits or spirits of wine. Basis of early finishes and Japanned work.

Three/French polish. Various types made from shellac base and toughening agents. Proprietary types: clear, button, orange, garnet, white, black and red. Soluble in methylated spirits and can be colored by spirit aniline dyes.

Four/Cellulose lacquer. Tougher, more water resistant finish than French polish used as a table-top varnish. Sometimes called enamel varnish or nitrocellulose. Soluble in recommended cellulose thinner. Acetone will remove it.

Five/Urethane polishes. Modern water-, heat- and spirit-resistant varnish. Kitchen furniture, outdoor types, table tops and so on.

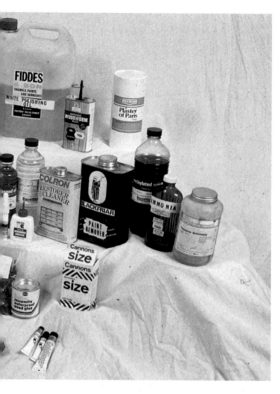

Above: Some of the materials used in furniture restoration. Top row, left to right: French polish, aniline spirit stain soluble in meths, white polishing oil, antiwoodworm fluid, plaster of Paris. Second row: White spirit, stained French polish, gold size, liquid drier, metal polish, car-body repair kit, oxalic acid bleach, super glue, PVA glue, raw linseed oil, turpentine, Colron restorer cleaner, paint remover, methylated spirits (denatured alcohol), ammonia, potassium dichromate. Bottom row: Shellac record, whiting, gold paints, gelatine, cabinet glue, stick shellac, urea glue, size. Front: Gold leaf, beeswax, artists oil paints, 'tube' gold.

Polyurethane, gloss or matt available.

*Six/*Acid-catalyzed lacquers. Plastic coating or plastic lacquer. Can make natural wood look like formica. Provides a heat-, moisture- and chemically-resistant film on modern pieces.

*Seven/*Patent knotting. For sealing resinous and 'weeping' knots prior to painting.

*Eight/*Teak oil. An oleoresinous varnish used as an alternative to linseed-oil finishing. It is more resistant than the latter.

*Nine/*Metal polish. For cleaning brass pulls and so on. It is sometimes handy for removing white water marks from French polish.

Resins and gums Sandarac resin, mastic gum, gum copal. Basis of some early varnishes. Used in making homemade varnishes and for stoppers and fillers. Dissolved in turpentine/linseed oil or benzine.

Fillers and stoppings

*One/*Proprietary wood filler. Plastic dough, wood dough. Oak, mahogany, walnut and so on available.

*Two/*Stick shellack. Available in variety of ready made shades. Homemade types produced by melting equal parts resin and beeswax with the addition of a few flakes of shellac for extra adhesion. Powder colors or oil stains added for color.

*Three/*Plaster of Paris and Whiting. Tinted with powder colors and linseed oil and used as a grain filler before polishing. Superfine whiting mixed with resin and gold size to make compo for ground work to gilded picture frames.

*Four/*Grain fillers and sealers. Various proprietary grain fillers, oak, mahogany and so on. Plasticized sealers for filling wood pores prior to polishing modern pieces.

Revivers These are used if cleaning with water and soap proves ineffective to revive shabby-looking wood as well as shellac and French polish.

1 part Methylated spirits	3 parts Vinegar
1 part Linseed oil	3 parts Linseed oil
1 part Paraffin	6 parts Methylated spirits
1 part best American Turpentine	$\frac{1}{2}$ part Butter of Antimony
1 part Vinegar	

Both above recipes will reamalgamate and redistribute glazed and cracked French polish. Methylated spirits acts as the polish softener while the other ingredients act as the vehicle and cleaner. The greater the quantity of methylated spirits, the more drastic the action. Used on raw wood surfaces, the oil content will tend to darken the wood.

Strippers

*One/*Household washing Soda. Dissolved in hot water this removes shellac-based varnishes but can raise the grain and darken some woods. Not recommended for antiques.

*Two/*Methylated spirits and steel wool. This is standard restorer's stripping kit. Tackle small areas at a time. Apply methylated spirits sparingly; once polish is soft, burnish off with steel wool.

*Three/*Dimethyl-Ketone (Acetone) and amyl acetate. These are effective strippers for cellulose-based lacquers and many modern finishes. They are flammable.

*Four/*Ammonia. Use the strong type from chemist, not diluted household variety. Removes old polish, asphaltum and milk paint, but darkens most hardwoods. It has an offensive smell and will 'burn' fingers.

*Five/*Chloroform. Dissolves heavy deposits of beeswax. Use in ventilated area.

*Six/*Thinners. Consult suppliers for appropriate type.

Seven/Proprietary paint stripper. Excellent types are available which will not raise grain or cause drastic darkening effects. Methylene chloride varieties will strip the toughest modern finishes.

All strippers have to be neutralized with the appropriate agent to prevent further action destroying subsequent finishes. Wipe off with methylated spirits, turpentine or water and vinegar depending on type and instructions.

Other useful materials and chemicals

One/Gold leaf. The paper-backed variety is easiest to handle. Books of 25 leaves are available for regilding furniture and picture frames.
Two/Bronze and gold powders. Various types are used for restoring Japanned furniture, picture frames and so on. They are bound with gold size.
Three/Degreasing agents. Carbontetrachloride and benzene for hard to glue oily woods such as rosewood and teak.
Four/Indian ink. Useful for pen and stencilled work.
Five/Surgical wool, dusters and cloths for polishing.
Although a few of the chemicals used in restoration are nontoxic it is best to treat the whole lot as poisonous. Handle them with care and avoid continuous skin contact. Bleaches, strippers, ammonia and other alkalies give off harmful vapors that will attack the flesh and lungs so use only in a well-ventilated workshop. Manufacturers instructions should be followed carefully and all bottles, cans and so on recorked after use. Even a badly corked Turpentine bottle can cause dizziness in a badly ventilated area. Naked flames should be kept well clear of the working area; steel wool burns like a dynamite fuse when set alight. Many chemicals cause side effects when brought into contact with certain materials. Powerful bleaches and acids will react with steel wool to produce a harmful vapor so it is best to paint them on rather than rub them on with the wool. Dyes, stains and colors are often only miscible in certain solutions and solvents, so before making up large batches, check that the base is of the correct type.

It is always a good idea to test the reaction of chemicals and stains on small unobtrusive areas of wood furniture before applying them in large quantities.

Metal fittings and fasteners

Metal fixing plates, angle brackets and the like are rarely used in furniture restoration. Surprising as it may seem, gluing is more effective and stronger in the long run. Screw-on metal straps initially appear to be a fast and convenient method of holding loose joints, bridging cracks and so forth but they should only be used as a last resort. Not only are they unsightly but quite often they can make matters worse. Even in severe cases of cracked table tops, for example, the recessed wooden butterfly or bowtie should be employed first. From the beginning of this century and even earlier many repairs to old furniture were carried out with these 'convenient' metal straps. Unfortunately in some cases they were not simply applied and screwed in place, frequently they were sunk and recessed into an otherwise perfect surface. Restoring furniture that is held together in this manner is extremely time consuming. Tenons that have become rounded and worn due to the continuous rubbing have to be fixed and the chopped-out graves for the metal straps have to be patched with homemade plywood for extra strength.

Other forms of fasteners such as screws and nails should be used

only where there is evidence of them in the original work, that is, they should be replaced if broken or damaged. Some joints are pegged with small dowelling, but they are never screwed and are infrequently nailed. Of course, badly made furniture of all ages makes abundant use of the nail. Seventeenth-century case furniture is often nailed. Bamboo and machine-shaped furniture from the late-nineteenth century is often jointed with long pin nails which can prove very trying to repair. Screws seem to be accepted to a greater extent in better class carpentry and cabinetwork but even their use is restricted to hidden places such as the supporting brackets on the underneath of furniture tops and the rubbed corner blocks to frame chairs. Many forms of nineteenth-century seat furniture have their arms secured to the back uprights with a plug-covered screw.

Original nuts and bolts and metal rods can be found as fasteners in the working parts of furniture. Wooden knuckle joints and the mechanical components to draw leaf tables are two examples. The backs of Thonet-type bentwood chairs are often secured to the seat with a nut and bolt, and many forms of outdoor and garden furniture have similar arrangements. All of these types have to be put back in position after cleaning with steel wool and a rust-proofing oil or, in cases of bad rusting and breakage, replaced with new fasteners of the same dimension.

Screws, nails and other forms of fasteners can be bought when needed; antique restorers usually have an extensive stock to supplement their collections of original old nails and screws salvaged from broken furniture. This 'magpie' approach is useful if you intend to restore a lot of furniture. Locks, hinges, old screws and nails can be saved from the furniture you buy for the wood. Apart from saving money, the use of these types is often far more in keeping with the restoration of old furniture.

Right: Furniture handles and fittings. 1–8: Iron 17th century and country types. 1, Butterfly hinge. 2 and 3, Snipe and strap hinge of the type found on antique coffers. 4 and 5, Early hinges, 5 is called a back flap and is used on drop-leaf tables and falls to bureaus from the 17th century onward. 6, Standard coffer lock. 7 and 8, Cock's head hinge for cupboard doors, decorated strap hinge exposed on lids of coffers and cupboards. 9–21: Mainly brass, late 17th- and early 18th-century types. 9, Iron drop. 10, Early wood pull. 11, Ring handle. 12–14, Inverted hearts and straight drops. 15 and 16, Brass back flap and cupboard butt hinge. 17–21, William and Mary and Queen Anne type pulls. 22–25, 18th-century rococo types. 22, Brass loop on pair of roses. 23–25, Various rococo escutcheons. 26–33, First phase of neoclassicism. 1760–1800, three geometric patterns. 29, Cast brass lion's head. 30–33, Second phase of neoclassicism 1800–1825. 30, Key hole anthemion. 31, Recessed brass handle. 32, Brass drawer knob. 33, Wooden pull without a threaded dowel. 34, Victorian wooden knob 1830–1890. 35–38, Late Victorian and Edwardian types. 39–41, Modern plastic or wood.

Below: Various old materials used by the professional restorer. Pieces of veneer, solid wood, oak, mahogany, box, ebony, bamboo, old tools and fittings.

WOOD in RESTORATION

Even in the twentieth century, with the developments of plastic and metal technology, wood remains the most important material in furniture making. Being in plentiful supply and almost ready for working has ensured wood's continuing success and popularity.

It is essential, therefore, that the restorer, like the cabinetmaker, has a technical understanding of wood. Many repairs to furniture involve nothing more than experimenting with recipes for dealing with different kinds of finishes, cleaning-up scratches and sorting out the less desirable marks of wear and use. Complicated repairs, however, such as replacing and repairing missing and damaged parts need an understanding of wood and how it works in furniture.

Identifying woods The first problem for the restorer is to establish what wood or woods the piece is made from. This is by no means an easy task: even the most experienced woodworker hesitates before making a positive identification. Certainly no photograph can effectively replace the experience of handling and working with wood. The ability to recognize woods is complicated for several reasons. No two trees of the same genus are identical in color or grain pattern. Climatic conditions, for example, can make oak from the Continent completely different to, say, English oak. The various methods of cutting boards from a tree produce all manner of differing grain patterns, figure and color. American red gum has a heartwood so different in color from the sapwood that until recently it was sold as two different woods, namely satin walnut and hazel pine. The effects of time and various stains, particularly on antique furniture, can cause endless speculation as to the nature of a wood. The bleaching effects of sunlight can make mahogany, walnut and cherry look remarkably similar. To add to the confusion, all types of cheap and featureless woods have been used to simulate exotic and expensive timber: gum, beech, deal and similar woods can be stained to look like rosewood, cherry or maple.

For easy reference, wood is usually divided under botanical headings of softwood and hardwood. Softwoods come from the trees bearing needle-pointed leaves, for example, the evergreens. Hardwoods come from the larger group of broad-leaved trees which can be further divided into equatorial types such as mahogany, rosewood, and teak and the temperate varieties like walnut, oak and sycamore. The names hardwood and softwood can be misleading because they do not always refer to the respective strengths of the wood. Within the hardwood range there are the soft and easily worked woods like lime, and dense and hard woods like ebony. The same range exists within the softwood family, soft pine and yew being two extremes.

Wood has to be seasoned before it can be used. Seasoning drives off the sap, leaving the timber in a stable condition where shrinkage will be minimal. For this reason trees are usually felled during the fall and winter when the sap is relatively inactive. Traditionally, seasoning is a slow, natural process taking three years or more but with the development of electric timber-drying kilns the process has been speeded up to a number of days.

For restoration purposes, it is important to place the wood under a broad generic heading and from there to establish a further classification. The oaks, mahoganies and walnuts can be recognized easily. Identifying the different varieties within a species takes a little more experience. For example, the finest member of the mahogany family, Spanish mahogany, is a far finer and darker wood than the pseudo-

Right: An English Windsor chair, circa 1820. It has an elm seat, ash legs, rungs and spindles, and birchwood hooped back and arms; a good example of how various woods are selected for their technical properties in furniture making.

Below: Identifying woods can prove to be a problem because of the various methods of cutting timber and the multitude of finishes, both natural and chemical, that can alter the appearance of furniture. This piece of plain-sawn oak has been coated with white paint and then stripped at some stage with caustic soda. The soda has reacted with the acids in the wood to produce a dull gray-brown look. Look underneath or inside furniture, where the wood can be seen in its natural state.

African types. A well-restored piece should appear to be untouched by repair work. As long as the 'mends' blend well, it does not matter if this is achieved by using a slightly different wood from the piece being restored. The best test is to look at an area unaffected by finish, patina and stain; under a table or inside a cabinet.

Grain, figure and color Having established the nature of the wood, try and match the direction of the grain and figure appearance of the missing pieces. The grain reflects the character and size of the growth rings in a tree. Each year a new layer of wood is produced by a layer of cells called the cambium, which produces bark on the outside and sapwood on the inner face. This growth appears on the face of boards as a series of parallel lines. The growth can be seen on the end of a board as a series of concentric rings. As a tree grows, additional layers are formed and the preceding sapwood gradually dies to form the fully developed center of the tree known as the heartwood or core. When sapwood is used to make furniture, the most common damage is woodworm or warping, particularly when softwoods like pine have been used. However, some hardwoods like beech and sycamore rarely show any difference between the sap and the core.

Some woods have a more striking grain pattern than others, and it often can be enhanced by the various methods of converting the log into planks. The cross-section of a tree will often reveal a series of lines that intersect the annual rings and radiate outward from the center. These are called medullary rays and appear as an attractive series of fleckings or splashes when the log is made into planks by the radially sawn method. Tangentially sawn timber produces some very striking grain patterns called figure.

Exotic grain patterns such as curl and burl tend to appear only in veneer form. This rare and expensive grain form is liable to warp and twist if cut in the solid.

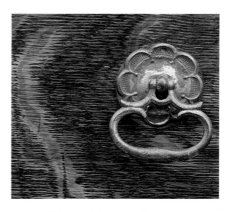

Above: Silver grain or medullary rays.

Below: 1, Annular growth rings and rays. Early craftsmen drove metal wedges down these natural cleavage lines in woods such as oak, ash and beech and, 2, the cake-like segments were then squared up. 3, Quarter sawing. A, B and D are less wasteful but C produces better figure. 4, The most economical method is plain sawing but here only the center planks show silver grain. 5, Tangentially sawn timber produces attractively marked boards. Each plank runs at a tangent to the annular rings. 6, Only the center board in plain sawing is unlikely to warp. Planks cut further from the center tend to warp because of differential reaction to drying out and humidity between the heartwood and sapwood side of the plank.

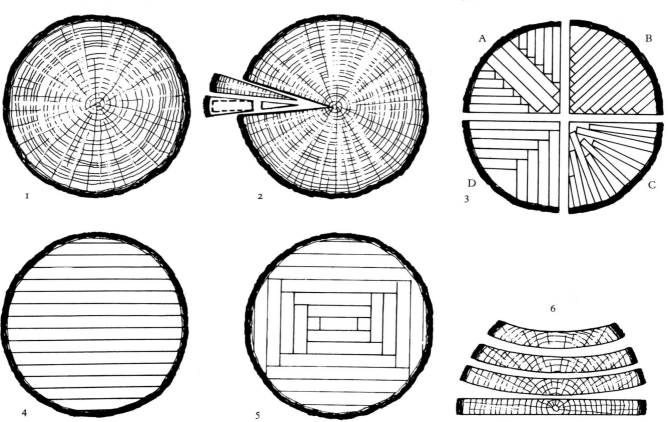

Technical properties and limitations The most important point to remember about wood is that despite the seasoning process, timber is still subject to expansion and contraction. By nature it is hydroscopic; it absorbs water from the air and expands in the process in damp conditions and in dry conditions moisture evaporates and the wood shrinks. Allowance has to be made for shrinkage across the grain – large areas of solid pine panelling are grooved into rebates so the wood can move freely. When you reassemble panelled pieces of furniture, therefore, it is important to avoid glue and nails – if the wood is unable to move cracks will develop along the grain of the plank.

Central heating causes considerable damage to furniture. The constant drying heat causes the furniture to go on shrinking until tremendous forces are set up: the wood shrinks to a size smaller than its original shape and cracks and warps appear in the sides and top of the piece. This type of damage is particularly difficult to cure. Damage by central heating can be avoided by placing humidifiers or bowls of water around the room. Alternatively, the absorbent, sponge-like quality of wood can be reduced by sealing the wood with wax or varnish. Antique furniture was rarely sealed, except on the exposed outer face of the piece. As a result, the exposed inner face of the boards are subject to movement and concave warping.

It is important to remember that wood is far stronger along the grain than across it. Knowing the strengths and weaknesses of the wood allows the restorer to select wood with the right grain direction for the job.

Below: An early-eighteenth-century joined oak child's chest. It is 2 foot 6 inches long × 1 foot 6 inches high. When restoring panelled constructions, avoid gluing the panels into their dados. Despite the relative stability of ply in comparison with solid wood, best-quality modern cabinets also have their panels 'free floated.' This allows the large, thin areas of wood to expand and contract, so they do not crack.

How to obtain wood for restoration One of the secrets of good restoration, particularly of antique furniture, is to use the right wood for replacing missing or damaged pieces. Replacements to antique furniture are far less conspicuous if old wood is used. A piece of furniture which is beyond restoration, called a breaker in the antique trade, is used solely for its wood. Technically, old wood has no special virtue. I have opened up a seventeenth-century oak beam, rescued from a demolished house, on the bandsaw to discover it has warped. The importance of old wood lies in its color and surface patination, which is extremely difficult to copy. As it is dark already, far less artificial coloring is needed. It can prove quite difficult to obtain old and broken furniture but it is definitely worth the expense to buy the odd piece now and again if you plan to restore antiques on a large scale. A piece of furniture has to be in a pretty dreadful condition to be broken up. A walnut chest-of-drawers, missing all its drawers, will provide a good supply of old wood and make for a better job restoring another walnut piece. But, a warning: the spiralling price

Left: The endless variety of grains and colors to be found on wood. Each sample has its bottom half coated with clear French polish, the top section is left in its natural state. Top row, left to right: Cuban mahogany, Honduras mahogany, African 'mahogany,' sapele 'mahogany,' walnut. Second row: Burl walnut, maple, teak, birch, rosewood. Third row: Beech, Australian silky 'oak,' poplar, ebony, ash. Fourth row: Tulipwood, padauk, cedar of Lebanon, cherry, English oak. Bottom row: Elm, bird's eye maple, East Indian satinwood, Swedish pine. black walnut.

Below: Beechwood showing its characteristic flecked-ray figure.

of antique furniture has made pieces that were not worth repairing 10 years ago a good financial proposition today. Modern veneer and solid wood can be obtained from wood supply firms.

Wood types

Hardwoods

APPLE (*Malus sylvestris*) Apple is hard and heavy. The color varies from pale yellow to pinkish-brown. Like most fruitwood, apple's use in furniture making is restricted by the size of the tree to small items, turned work and inlay. It works well if tools are kept sharp, though care is needed because the grain can run in opposite directions. Acceptable substitutes for apple are beech, poplar and other fruitwoods. Light-colored spirit or oil stains sealed with beeswax or shellac color apple wood well. A close-grained hardwood, apple takes a high natural shine.

ASH (*Fraxinus* species) Ash is a tough, flexible wood used more for its technical properties than its appearance. It is a moderately light wood varying in color from grayish white to pale brown. It bends and works well and was used in England and North America for simple country furniture. New replacements are difficult to color, so old wood should be used where possible. New wood can be aged by sealing the open grain first. Stain made from saphaltum dissolved in turpentine to a paste consistency can then be painted on and stripped on with wire wool when dry. Subsequent burnishing with a hard smooth object will further close up the grain. Some cuts of elm and chestnut look similar to ash and can be used as alternatives.

BASSWOOD *see* Lime.

BEECH (*Fagus* species) Beech is one of the most commonly used hardwoods. It is a hard and heavy wood, even grained and marked with a flecked figure. The color is yellowish brown, occasionally pink when steamed. Beech is rarely used as a finished cabinet wood. Carcass work, structural components and wooden mechanical joints such as swing gates are made from this wood. It is often used to imitate more expensive woods. In the past quantities of beech were used in country furniture, caned chairs and painted pieces. Water stains work well on beech, though resin-based stains like teak oil are ideal for antique repairs. Despite its hard-wearing properties, beech gets heavily wormed and sometimes has to be replaced. Ash and hickory can be used as alternatives.

BUTTERNUT *see* Walnut

BIRCH (*Betula* species) Birch is a close-grained and fairly heavy wood, soft-brown in color and similar to maple in character. Like mahogany, it radically altered the course of furniture design. The Austrian firm of Thonet pioneered the concept of elaborate curved work in furniture, by using birchwood's ability to bend well when steamed. By the late nineteenth century birch rod dowelling was fast replacing the mortise and tenon as a quick and less costly means of joining cheap furniture. Large amounts of this wood are used for modern plywood. Birch works well and finishes to such a fine lustrous surface that it is often used to imitate cherry and maple. Some of the knotty and curly varieties make excellent veneer for fine furniture.

BOXWOOD (*Buxus sempervirens*) Box is a heavy, hard and close-grained wood. Its use for furniture is limited to decorative inlay, stringing and banding. Pieces can be purchased in various sizes from specialist wood suppliers. With age box goes a deep yellow. This can be simulated with a strong mixture of yellow and oak spirit stains.

CHERRY (*Prunus* species) Cherrywood is the finest of the fruit-

Below: Canadian birch. Curly varieties make excellent substitutes for West Indian satinwood, cherry and maple in restoration.

wood family. It has a dense, even-natured grain and varies in color from the cream of the sap to the dark-red-brown of the heartwood. It is specially known to North America for fine furniture and is called American mahogany. It works well, despite its toughness, and finishes to a beautiful shine. Apart from its use in the solid, cherry has been popular for turned items, decorative inlay and for legs of modern factory-made furniture with faked cherrywood tops. Cherry stains well. Poplar and fruitwood can be used as substitutes.

CHESTNUT (*Aesculus and Castanea* species) Of the two varieties of this wood, the horse and the sweet chestnut, the latter is a far more durable wood. Slightly lighter than oak and with a reddish-brown coloring, it has been used in the past for country furniture, panelling and drawer linings. Due to the American chestnut blight early in this century antique pieces now have a rarity value. Elm and ash look similar in certain cuts, though oak has closer working properties to chestnut. Chestnut accepts stain well and has been used in the past to simulate oak and walnut.

EBONY (*Diospyros* species) Ebony is a highly prized cabinet wood. It has a dense black color and is extremely heavy. It requires a great deal of care to work as it is very brittle. In the past the artificial sort, called 'German ebony,' was used. This can be made by steeping woods like sycamore, beech or fruitwood in blue/black aniline dyes dissolved in alcohol. Black leather shoe dye is also excellent for this purpose. Olive oil will revive shabby looking ebony.

ELM (*Ulmus* species) Elm is much used for varieties of English country furniture. It is pale brown in color but darkens with age. The most important aspect of elm is its fibrous and interlocking grain, which make it ideal for wooden chair seats. Legs can be fixed in without any chance of the wood splitting. The hardwearing nature of this wood makes it ideal for table tops and for mechanical joints in furniture. Unfortunately it can warp badly and is extremely vulnerable to rot and woodworm attack. Structural components and working parts usually require some attention. Spirit based stains and waxes are normally used for elm. Regrettably many antique pieces end up heavily French polished.

GUM (*Liquidambar styraciflua*) Gum wood has a close and even grain. It is pale brown in color with a darker core. At times it is marked with black streaks. Gum looks very similar to whitewood (American poplar). Gum works and stains very well. It is popular in North America for mass-production furniture as it can be made to look like expensive woods. It is excellent for carving but tends to warp easily.

HICKORY (*Carya* species) This wood resembles ash and is used for much the same purposes. It is slightly tougher and harder than ash, close grained and nearly white in color. Hickory is not an easy wood to work because it splinters easily, however its flexibility and resilience make it good for bentwood furniture. Many painted chairs from colonial New England were made from this wood. Hickory is not durable in moist or exposed conditions as it is liable to attack from fungi and worms. It stains well and can be used for faking mahogany and walnut.

HOLLY (*Ilex aquifolium*) Holly is a close-grained white wood which is heavy and dense. It has been used since the seventeenth century for inlay, veneer and turned work. Its most important quality is that it takes all manner of stains. Restoration normally involves replacing stringing and inlay. Most of the pale-colored, close-grained and featureless hardwoods can be used if holly is not available.

Top left: Cherry.
Center left: Macassar, or striped ebony.
Note how the wood darkens and almost loses its stripe with a single coat of stain-free French polish.
Below left: Freshly cut English elm. A more characteristic example of the wide and irregular growth pattern of this wood can be seen in the Windsor chair seat on page 55.

LIME (*Tilia* species) Lime or Basswood, as it is called in the United States, is another of the featureless woods used in modern furniture to simulate more expensive and exotic types. It is almost white when first cut but darkens to a yellow-brown with age. It is one of the finest carving woods, having an even texture and cutting sharp in all directions. It stains well.

MAHOGANY Mahogany has many technical properties, besides its rich red color and superb figure, that makes it a superb cabinet timber. Its metal-like strength and resistance to warping and decay has made it popular for fine furniture for more than 250 years. It is useful to remember when it comes to identifying the various genus of mahogany that the darker and heavier the wood (in its natural state) the better will be its quality and the older will be its use in furniture. Basically there are three main groups:

One/SPANISH MAHOGANY This is a broad term that covers the dark-red genus of *Swietenia mahogani*. The first type to be used was the dark, straight-grained San Domingan variety, first imported into England on a large-scale in the 1720s. A featureless wood, it was used mainly for pieces in the solid. By about 1750 the more highly figured Cuban varieties came into use both in veneer form and in the solid.

It is difficult to get hold of Spanish mahogany these days. For antique repairs the lighter colored Central American types, like Honduras, can be darkened by chemical staining with bichromate of potash. Cuban mahogany has a white deposit in the grain which distinguishes it from the Central American varieties.

Two/CENTRAL AMERICAN MAHOGANY (*Swietenia macrophylla*) This is a lighter and softer variety of mahogany, orange in color and sometimes superbly figured. It can be found in use from the late-eighteenth century onward. Being a soft wood in comparison, many antique pieces get heavily scratched and dented. The fine-figured cuts can usually be found in veneer form while the straight-grained wood is mainly employed for carcass work and sides of cabinets.

Three/PSEUDO MAHOGANIES By the 1870s similar woods were used to supplement the dwindling supplies of true mahogany. African Mahogany (*Khaya ivorensis*) is the best of this group. It is

Below: Cuban mahogany can be distinguished from the other mahoganies by the white deposit in its grain. Beware of the late 19th-century technique of filling the grain of cheaper mahoganies with plaster of Paris.
Below center: Honduras mahogany or 'baywood.'
Below right: African 'mahogany.'

lighter, less attractively marked and not as strong as the Central American. In its natural state it has a pinkish tinge and an open-pored grain. Other varieties of 'mahogany' are the commercial types such as Meranti, sapele, utile and makore. These form the main source for mass-produced and reproduction furniture.

Mahogany is a difficult wood to work and restore. The multitude of cuts and finishes can cause problems in matching the timber. Faded wood is difficult to replace, as bleaching leaves the wood with no depth. The Spanish types can be very brittle to work but they finish beautifully. Frequently the grain needs to be filled on the pseudo types before polishing.

OAK (*Quercus* genus) Despite the preference at one period or another for the mahoganies, walnuts and rosewoods, oak has always been extensively used for country furniture for carcass work and as a cabinet wood in its own right. Its color can vary from yellow to pale brown, depending on the species and conditions of growth. Technically, oak is strong, reliable and durable. It is not an easy wood to work but for the purposes of restoration it is one of the simplest for making invisible repairs. This aspect of oak, coupled with the fact that most people are prepared to accept heavy signs of wear and tear on old oak furniture, has made it one of the faker's favorite woods. Oak has an open-pored grain and takes all kinds of finishes, the most well-known of which is the antique finish, favored by the Victorians for reproduction furniture. Spirit stains and beeswax polish should be used for antique pieces requiring minor repairs.

PEAR (*Pyrus communis*) Pearwood is very similar to apple, both in grain and color. Its one outstanding quality is that it carves well in all directions. Much of it is used for inlay work and for simulating ebony.

POPLAR *see* Whitewood

ROSEWOOD (*Dalbergia* species) There are two main varieties of this hard and exotic wood. The finest is Brazilian which has a dense nature and a coarse open grain. Its color is pale brown with black streaks. Many American pieces from the Empire period to the present day are made from this type. Other varieties are tulipwood (not to be confused with American whitewood which is sometimes called tulipwood) which is beautifully striped with purple bands on a tan background. Kingwood is the heaviest of the rosewood family and has a very thin stripe. East Indian rosewood is darker in color and not so distinctively marked. When newly cut it is black but fades with time to a pale honey. Rosewood is an obstinate and difficult wood to work. It is very splintery and because of the oily nature of the wood, it is hard to get a good gluing surface. Parts that require rejoining should be degreased with carbon tetrachloride. In veneer form rosewood has the tendency to develop minute cracks and to break off in jagged sections. Replacing damaged areas on faded furniture requires a stock of old and patinated wood. No amount of chemical bleaching can achieve this effect. For solid repairs the orange-colored Central American mahoganies should be used and the stripe simulated with bichromate of potash. Care and patience is necessary when stripping faded rosewood as it is very easy to cut through to the darker wood that lies just under the surface. If staining is required the spirit-based types should be employed. Shellac and French polish are the traditional finishes for rosewood. Prior to this the grain should be filled.

SATINWOOD The two varieties of satinwood are named after the parts of the world they come from. The West Indian variety

Left: English oak. Elm and oak are easily confused, particularly antique wood. A sure test is to look under or inside the piece. Unfinished elm has a pinky gray cast while unfinished antique oak is often nut-brown or gray-brown in color. The presence of medullary rays would also indicate that the piece in question is oak and not elm.
Left center: Rosewood.
Left below: East Indian satinwood.

(*Fagara flava*) has a nice golden color and a close rich figure. The East Indian variety is more lemon colored and comparatively free of markings apart from a faint longitudinal stripe. White-colored glue has to be used for repair work, otherwise glue lines can be unsightly. Birch, boxwood and maple make good substitutes when colored with spirit stains.

MAPLE (*acer* genus) The best wood of the Maple family comes from the Northern Maple (*acer saccharum*). The majority of maple furniture is American, though veneered pieces, particularly of the bird's eye variety, can be found in English nineteenth-century furniture. Maple is a tough, moderately heavy and fine-grained timber. Its color varies from cream to yellow. As a hard-wearing and fine-finishing wood it is ideal for fine-quality cabinet work. New replacements to maple have to be finely sanded before staining. Imperfections in the surface show up very easily. Shellac is a good sealer for this wood, followed by a wax or French polish finish.

TEAK (*Tectona grandis*) Teak is a heavy hardwood, dark brown in color. It is an extraordinary wood to work: when freshly cut it has an odd waxy texture and a peculiar leather-like smell. It cuts well but has a deposit of white phosphate of lime in its grain that can blunt saws and chisels. Teak, like oak, darkens on exposure. It is one of the most durable, decay-resistant and strongest timbers available but due to its dull appearance and weight it is only recently that it has been selected for making furniture in the west. In restoration work teak can prove difficult; like rosewood it is hard to glue and impossible to bleach. Teak oil is the standard finish for modern pieces.

TULIPWOOD *see* Rosewood and Whitewood

WALNUT (*Juglans* species) Walnut is considered one of the finest of the cabinet woods. The timber is fairly hard but easy to work and usually beautifully marked with a varied figure that is hard to match in other woods. The two common types are European walnut (*Juglans regia*) and American black walnut (*Juglans nigra*). Both have been used extensively in English furniture from the sixteenth century. The American variety is a much darker wood and is often called Virginian red walnut. It can be found used in pieces made in the original 13 states. The American white walnut (*Juglans cinerea*),

Below: Bird's eye maple.
Below center: Teak.
Below right: Tulipwood, a member of the rosewood family.

sometimes called butternut, is rarely used for fine furniture. Its popularity is restricted to stained reproduction pieces like Victorian imitation walnut chairs and sideboards. Walnut has always been an expensive wood, consequently much of it is converted into veneer, particularly the finely marked varieties. Quite often pseudo-varieties are used, such as satin walnut or American gum. Other walnut types are West African and Pacific walnut. For repairs to antique walnut, old wood should be used. Water or spirit stains should be used for coloring walnut. Shellac or oil polishes such as boiled linseed oil work well on later pieces but beeswax is the best for antiques that have been stripped of their shellac or natural finish.

WHITEWOOD, AMERICAN (*Liriodendron tulipfera*) American whitewood is more commonly called poplar or yellow poplar in the United States. It is in fact not a true poplar but comes from the American tulip tree. To add to the confusion it is sometimes called tulipwood but has none of the characteristics of the real tulipwood which is a member of the rosewood family. Whitewood varies in color from white to soft brown. It is quite a hard, featureless wood with a fine and even texture. Its ability to stain well makes it ideal for all forms of modern and reproduction furniture.

Softwoods

DEAL The term deal covers a multitude of softwoods such as pine, larch, fir, hemlock and spruce. The colors and technical properties of these woods vary enormously, however they are usually sold in secondhand and antique shops under the broad heading of pine. All of these types have the advantage of being cheap and easy to work. In the past they were used for country furniture, carcass work and for painted, veneered and Japanned pieces. With the current craze for pale-colored woods numerous Victorian types have their veneer of hardwood removed to make them more saleable. Replacing missing moldings and broken parts of 'pine furniture' requires a careful selection of the right wood for the job. Repairs to pitch pine, with its distinctive orange stripes, will be all too obvious if a featureless species like yellow pine is used. Darker woods are the easiest types to invisibly repair since the staining process covers any minor discrepancies in color and grain. Pale woods like pine, maple and satinwood do not allow for the use of heavy stains to obscure and blend in repair work. Spirit stains and spirit-based waxes are excellent for pine and deal furniture. The permanent oil-based stains can be too fierce, leaving the wood with very little depth. Kitchen furniture needs to be waxed regularly or sealed with a water-resistant varnish, such as polyurethane, otherwise the wood tends to fir up with wear.

CEDAR Many varieties of true and false cedar have been used for furniture, mainly in the form of carcass work, drawer linings and panelling. The wood is pale orange in color, somewhat like mahogany, and usually marked with a distinctive striped figure. The West Indian type (*Cedrela ordorata*) is used for the inner casings of wardrobes and for furniture where clothes are stored. The aromatic smell and oily nature of the wood make it ideal for keeping all forms of insects and moths away. Cedar wood bruises easily. Dents and score marks can sometimes be raised with a moderately hot iron and a damp cloth. Old cigar boxes provide a useful supply of this wood for repair work. Shellac or French polish are good finishes for cedar as they seal in the natural oils and enhance the grain features.

YEW WOOD (*Taxus baccata*) When worked and finished well, yew is one of the most beautiful of woods. Its extremely fine and dense nature makes it one of the heaviest of the softwoods. The

Left: English walnut.
Left center: Black walnut.
Left below: Cedar of Lebanon.

swirling grain pattern and high natural shine of yew take on a glass-like patination, particularly in antique furniture, that is hard to match. Most pieces are of European origin. From the seventeenth century onward it was used for small furniture and for bentwood chairs of the Windsor type. It is one of the few softwoods that bends well when steamed. Care is needed when working this wood as the grain can be very irregular. Oil stains can be used to simulate the dark orange-brown of antique yew. If yew is unobtainable, close-grained cedar can be used as a substitute. Wax polish is the best finish for this wood.

Manmade and manufactured boards The use of natural wood substances in the manufacture of synthetic particle and laminated products is mostly confined to the twentieth century. These proprietary boards now provide a cheap substitute for solid wood. However, as far back as the early 1700s a few examples of composite materials are found. One of these is 'marblewood,' which is produced by compressing a mass of wood shavings, chippings and glue into a block, rather similar to the modern method of making chipboard. The result was then turned on the lathe or sliced to produce a veneer similar in figure to burl or pollard wood. The most basic of laminates can also be found in the curved surfaces of antique cabinet work, where strips of wood are glued together in an arc and then veneered over. This method avoided the brittle nature of short grain.

With the technical developments and the beginnings of the mechanization of the furniture trade in the mid-nineteenth century, perhaps the most important innovation in this field was introduced by John Belter (1804–1863) who replaced Duncan Phyffe as New York's best-known cabinetmaker. Belter was obsessed with elaborately curved shapes but hindered at the same time by his favorite material – rosewood, which is short-grained and not strong enough

Below: A marquetry table with ormolu mounts and porcelain plaques, mid-nineteenth century. It is a fine example of how materials and wood are used for both a naturalistic and geometric effect.

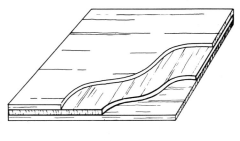

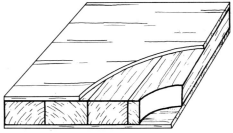

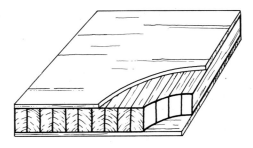

Above: Three of the most common laminated boards. Top, equal layer plywood. Center, blockboard. Above, laminboard.

Left: A rosewood chair attributed to John Belter, circa 1845. Belter's standard laminating process involved gluing together 6 to 8 layers of wood to form panels or strips. Each layer was one-sixteenth of an inch thick and was laid so that its grain ran at a right angle to the next layer, as in the laminates above. The finished laminate was steamed in a mold to bend it to the desired shape. Florid neorococo decorations were then carved. Excessively elaborate and 'deep' shapes were also carved from solid wood and applied later.

for use in curved work. In 1847 he patented a process which allows as many as 16 panels or strips of rosewood to be laminated together in such a way that they can be steam bent into the required shape.

The success of Belter's laminating and ply process led to all kinds of developments in composite materials and production-line techniques. In fact many historians mark this point as the beginning of the decline of sound cabinet skills in favor of cheaper materials and faster methods. Be that as it may, manufactured boards have none of the problems associated with solid wood, such as shrinkage, splitting and warping.

Repairs to plywood and synthetic boards is a fairly lengthy process. In some cases where damage is severe it is often cheaper to buy a complete new board of the same type and dimension. Chipped veneer facings and edges can be repaired and glued back with any of the modern urea adhesives.

PLYWOOD This is one of the first types to be used for mass production furniture. From early in this century it was used extensively for panelling, drawer bottoms, carcass-backs and for any large area where solid wood would prove too expensive and prone to warping and extensive shrinkage. In its simplest and earliest form plywood is made up from three layers of wood, the center layer having its grain running at right angles to those on either side. Such an arrangement makes it as strong in its width as in its length. Later developments produced stout heart and five ply which are even stronger and more reliable. Plywood can be bought in thicknesses varying from $\frac{1}{8}$ inch to 1 inch. Where these boards are used as a finished surface they are faced with a veneer of expensive hardwood like oak and mahogany. Cheaper woods, such as birch, ash and Douglas fir are used for the other layers.

BLOCKBOARD This is used mainly for cheap furniture, kitchen fitments, book shelves and so forth. It is built up with an inner core of numerous strips of 1-inch wide softwood, laid edge to edge and then covered on both sides with a thick hardwood veneer whose grain runs at right angles to the core. Thickness varies from $\frac{1}{2}$ inch to $1\frac{1}{2}$ inches.

LAMINBOARD Laminated board is the sturdiest and most reliable of composite mediums and is used for high-class modern furniture. It is made in much the same way as blockboard with the exception of the core strips, which are never more than $\frac{1}{4}$ inch wide. In both laminboard and blockboard the grain of the core strips is reversed in gluing.

Particle and Chipboard Chipboard is made by compressing wood chips together under pressure using modern synthetic resins as the bonding agent. The cheapest variety of board, it is frequently used in the production of the less desirable pieces for the lower end of the market. It has a tendency to warp so a supporting framework has to be used in cabinet backs and veneered surface work. Thickness varies from $\frac{1}{2}$ inch to $\frac{3}{4}$ inch.

When working any of the above manmade boards, it helps to cut them exactly to size first time. Owing to the opposing grain directions and high resin content, subsequent trimming with a plane or rasp can cause the edges to fray and chip. A circular saw fitted with a tungsten carbide or veneer and laminate blade saves a lot of time and provides a clean edge for veneering or lipping with a hardwood facing. Naturally, none of these boards should be used in the repair of antique funiture although they can provide a useful standby for missing drawer bottoms until a piece of solid wood can be found.

THE ART of RESTORATION

In its truest sense, restoration is not only a craft but an attitude – a way of approaching damaged furniture that differs completely from ordinary repair work. It is an attempt to conserve and restore pieces back to their original state with an allowance for the effects of time. Many people confine this approach to the repair of antique furniture. However to my way of thinking the simple rules of restoration should apply to any piece of furniture, irrespective of whether it dates from 1660 or 1960. So much good furniture has been ruined in the past by people allowing their personality and taste to dominate their approach to repair work. Original polishes have been stripped off, pieces have had legs removed or cut off to make them fit into particular rooms, old surfaces have been sanded down because they were unfashionable at the time and a whole host of other 'repairs,' 'improvements' and alterations have been carried out. Until recently fashion was largely responsible for this, and while you might think it unimportant to apply the rules of restoration to a 20- or 30-year-old chair, for example, it must be remembered that much the same attitude was taken in the past by one generation or another altering the furniture of the previous period to suit their taste. A good illustration of this is the chest of drawers. The Victorians and Edwardians, with their preference for wooden knobs, removed the brass handles off Regency and early nineteenth-century pieces and drilled large holes through the fronts of the drawers in order to fit their preferred type of pull. Forty or so years ago brass fittings came back into fashion and not only were the brasses replaced on the Regency pieces but wooden knobs were changed on many Victorian examples. Unfortunately everyone got a bit carried away and included in these changes were some fine examples of Sheraton-style and Regency chests that were *originally* made with wooden knobs! Nowadays the antique trade would much rather pay a better price for something in its original state. How long the present attitude of conserving as much of the original as possible lasts remains to be seen. Hopefully it is here to stay since the rules of restoration are static and unchangeable whatever the current crazes and fads might be.

Unfortunately furniture is still altered to make it more saleable, especially the popular types of furniture which are consequently expensive. With the recent craze for light-colored woods such as pine many mahogany-veneered Victorian pieces end up stripped of their original wood covering so as to expose the pale carcass wood. All of these types end up with the label eighteenth-century colonial!

During the early years of this century, when restoration was in its infancy, some antique furniture of the late eighteenth and nineteenth century was appallingly treated. As people moved into smaller houses with lower ceilings large pieces of furniture such as chest on chests and sideboards were made smaller and more saleable. Clean and bright furniture was in fashion, so many natural shellac and French-polished surfaces which were only slightly marred were stripped off completely and repolished. This resulted in many pieces loosing their patination which had taken years to produce. These days a polish reviver and some careful patching is all that is used to restore a slightly damaged surface to its former condition.

The first rule of restoration is therefore to do as little as possible in the way of repairs. A step by step process is used – starting with moderate techniques and working up the scale to more severe techniques. If, for example, you were faced with a damaged and dirty

Below and bottom: Old furniture surfaces can easily be destroyed by heavy stripping or careless use of sandpaper. The 17th-century oak (below) shows exposed worm channels. It is very easy when levelling a replacement patch to cut through the surrounding surface and expose these unsightly holes. The 18th-century Honduras mahogany (bottom) with curl figure shows how patina and fading are lost forever by using sandpaper on antique surfaces. The stripped section is lighter in color, but one application of a clear wax or French polish will turn it deep red.

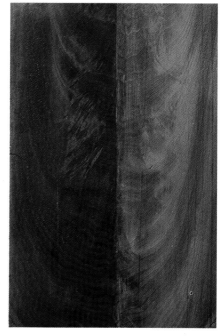

surface you might try a damp and slightly soaped cloth first. If this does not work, try to blend the finish back together with a polish reviver. Only if all else fails should stripping be undertaken. As you gain more experience in restoration you will learn to gauge what is going to work best without having to go through the step-by-step process. Even here the experienced restorer will do a series of small tests before he decides on the final course of action as there are a multitude of different finishes for furniture.

The older a piece of furniture is, then the more acceptable is the damage. Where the restorer would remove the scratches on a nine-teenth-century piece of mahogany, for example, similar damage or marks of wear on an oak piece from the seventeenth century are deemed acceptable. Antiques would loose a lot of their appeal if they looked immaculate and unmarked.

While it is natural for the cabinetmaker to allow his personality to show in his work, the restorer cannot afford such luxuries. He has to

Below: 19th-century walnut. When abrasive paper is used instead of a cabinet scraper, for levelling a patch repair to antique walnut, the result is disastrous. The paper cuts clean through the patina either side of the patch and no amount of chemical bleaching will restore this.

Bottom: This chair is over 150 years old but it is quite worthless as an antique, because it has been dipped in a stripping tank. The wood has furred up and the salts from the caustic have come to the surface. The picture alongside shows a similar Windsor chair with its original paint intact.

subjugate his own personality so that at the end of the job the piece is unaffected by his personal idiosyncracies. Where the cabinetmaker would quite rightly shudder at the sight of butt and nailed drawers in an antique chest, the restorer accepts them as part of the nature of the piece.

Finally, an awareness of how wood works in furniture is essential. Plywood and modern laminboards have none of the characteristics of solid wood, they are relatively static materials and consequently do not require such careful handling. Wood in the solid is constantly on the 'move,' owing to varying heat and moisture levels, and this factor has to be taken into consideration. When panelled constructions are put back together, for example, the boards must not be glued into their rabbets otherwise they will split when they start to move. Similarly, different woods react in different ways to stains and chemicals. Some do not swell over much when water stain is used while others tend to fur up unless a spirit or oil stain is used.

A few of the following tips might prove useful to the beginner to restoration. There is usually a stage in the work where the piece looks far worse than when you started, particularly if you have to dismantle something to effect a repair. You have to grit your teeth and patiently work through this middle ground. If you are restoring the piece for someone else it can help to lock the workroom door to avoid giving the owner a heart attack! Sometimes it is easy to know what to do and how to go about it, but inevitably an odd piece defies an easy solution. In such instances it is usually best to stop work and return to the piece the next day. An outside opinion, even from someone who is not familiar with restoration, can provide some surprisingly good results. Restoration involves a great deal of close up work so it can help to stand back occasionally and view the piece as whole to see how the repairs are blending in. Before starting work, the piece should have as many of its detachable parts removed as possible. This allows an ease of working and will prevent further damage to otherwise sound components. Table tops can be unscrewed for example and put to one side. At this stage it is always a good idea to have a look inside drawers and compartments for bits of missing veneer, moldings and handles that have come off and been placed there for safe keeping. Nothing is more annoying than finding an original piece of wood after you have made an unnecessary replacement. Where veneer is lifting and cracking off, it is a good idea to put the bits in the zip-up type of transparent plastic bags used by coin collectors so they do not get lost. If you put these bits on the workbench they usually get lost in the wood shavings and finding them again is very difficult. Putting furniture back together again is facilitated by marking all the respective matching joints with colored tape before dismantling; despite initial similarities each joint will have been subjected to varying degrees of shrinkage and will only fit back into its original housing. A useful technique in restoration is to try and imagine yourself in the shoes of the person who made the piece originally. Have a good look at everything and ask yourself why such and such a joint or piece of wood was used and whether the maker

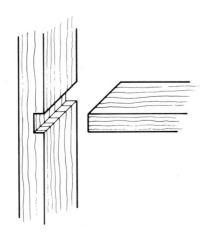

Below: The dado, or housing joint, used in carcass furniture for the dividers to drawers. This joint takes the weight of heavy drawers extremely well, since the housing provides a step which resists downward pressure.
Below right: The scarfed joint or long splice. This is not a cabinet joint, but is one of the most common repair joints.

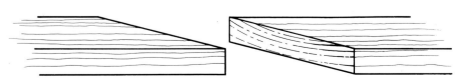

was an amateur, carpenter, joiner or cabinetmaker. The modern mass-produced piece usually lacks this kind of 'personality.' Where whole sections are missing and you have nothing to work from it is handy to have a furniture pattern or history book available so that your replacements will be in keeping with the style and age of the piece. Professional restorers rely heavily on a thorough knowledge of the techniques and styles peculiar to certain periods; this way they avoid making anachronisms.

While it is easy to apply the rules of restoration to furniture that is obviously all original, it can seem pointless when you come across the piece that has been mistreated or is 75 percent fake. Here you either have to avoid the piece in the first place or try and put it right without damaging it even further. It is often best to avoid these pieces as they can prove extremely trying. Similarly, when viewing furniture with restoration in mind, estimate the time you think it is going to take to repair and then double it. Sometimes you get a nice surprise and the job is done in a matter of hours, but this is unusual. Quite often someone will have hammered nails into joints and so forth, and you will notice these when you start work or try to get a joint apart. Bad repairs take a long time to sort out.

For most furniture restoration proceed as follows:
One/Clean the piece with a damp cloth to reveal damage, grain direction, wood type and previous repairs.
Two/Examine damaged areas.
Three/Remove sound parts that can be unscrewed or lifted off to avoid damaging them.
Four/Dismantle the affected areas if necessary to facilitate repairs.
Five/Carry out carpentry and ground work repairs.
Six/Reassemble with a 'dry' run before gluing and clamping.
Seven/Do veneer and surface repairs according to age and type.
Eight/Stain, match and polish if required.

You might change the order sometimes; it is sometimes easier to do the staining and polishing process before reassembly, particularly on pieces of a fancy nature with hard to get at surfaces.

Finally while conservation is an intrinsic part of restoration work in that moderate methods are essential, do not let a piece of furniture scare you out of starting repairs. Have a go with the methods prescribed, avoid drastic techniques like sanding surfaces or heavy stripping and if you get stuck consult an expert. It is a fascinating and extremely diverse craft which can lead you to being master of many trades.

Right : Types of joints. 1, Joiner's mortise and tenon found on 17th-century and country pieces. Dry pegged. 2, Carpenter's mortise and tenon. 17th century and country. Dry and glued. 3, Cabinetmaker's mortise and tenon. 18th century. Always glued. 4, Butt. Straight and right angle. Glued and/or nailed. 5, Rabbet. Straight and right angle. Cheap pieces from all ages. Glued and/or nailed. 6, Twin dowel. Victorian onward. Always glued. 7, Wedged. Farmhouse and Windsor. Dry or glued. 8, Finger or box. Straight and right angle. Mainly 19th century. Always glued. 9, Tongu and groove. Straight and right angle. Mainly 19th century onward. Glued. 10, Through dovetails. Mid-17th century onward. Glued 11, Lapped dovetails. 18th century onward. Glued. 12, Single dovetail. Joining table frame to legs. Also used in early drawer constructions.

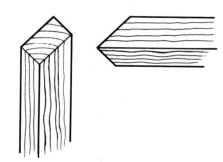

Below: A miter joint, used from the 17th century onward. Glued and/or nailed.

Bottom left: Rubbed glue blocks. Found underneath antique case furniture.
Bottom: Halved joint. Cheap plywood panel frame.

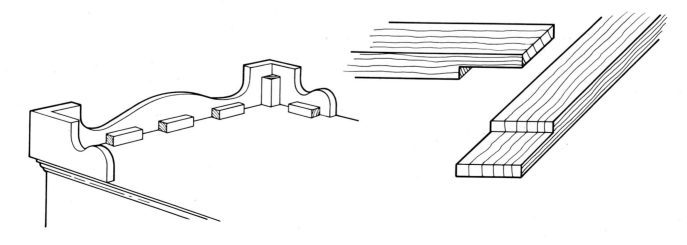

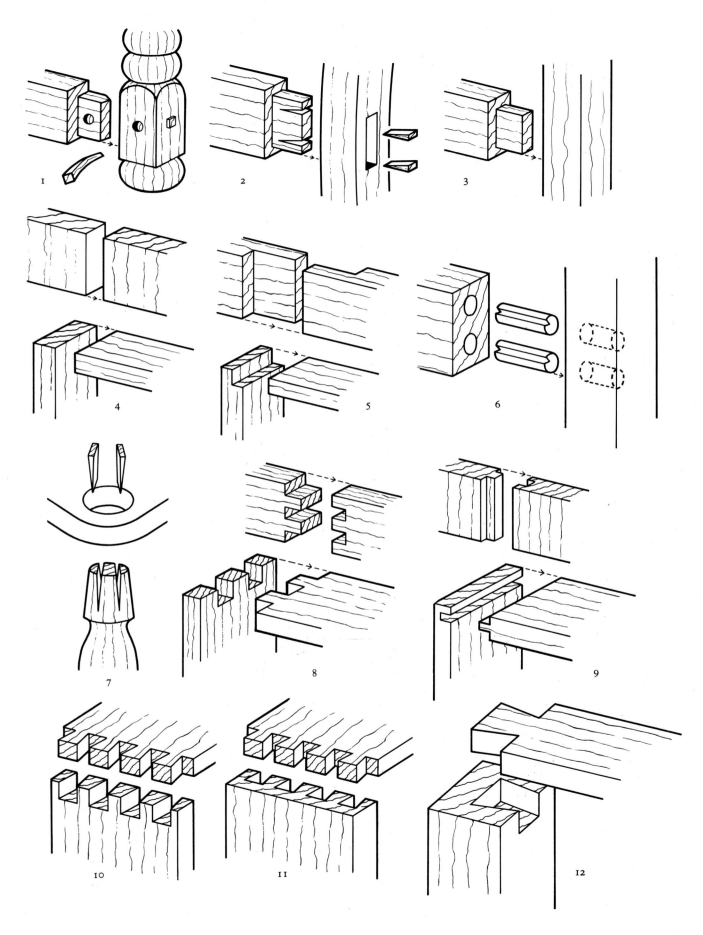

CHAIRS and STOOLS

Chairs and stools seem to suffer more damage than any other form of furniture. They are subject to all kinds of stresses and strains for which they were not designed. The most common misuse occurs when people lean back on the two back legs. Inevitably, such bad treatment results in the joints, particularly in older types, breaking off or coming loose from their housings, eventually causing the whole chair to fall apart. Since each part of a chair is designed to work in conjunction with its fellows, if one component breaks the remaining sound parts have to take on an extra workload. If repairs are not done immediately, all kinds of troublesome damage will occur.

Chair restoration is complicated by the seemingly endless variety of designs and shapes chairs have. However, for the moment ignore all the different makes of chair and concentrate instead on the three basic methods of construction. Since this book is dealing primarily with wooden furniture, cast-aluminium and polypropylene varieties by designers like Charles Eames and Robin Day will be excluded.

Stool, kitchen and Windsor chair Viewed structurally, these chairs are simply stools, composed of four legs joined into a seat with the back added as a separate unit. If the back were to be removed the base would still hold together as a stool. The generic term Windsor is often used as an example of how the stool developed into the chair over the centuries. The majority of components will be turned and linked together by the dowel-and-socket method of joinery. Upholstery is rarely used; the whole chair including the seat is solid wood.

Frame chair The frame chair differs from its predecessor in one fundamental way: the back legs, instead of finishing in the seat, extend upward in the form of uprights to make the back, and join up with the top or cresting rail. Common varieties include the bedroom and dining room types. All frame chairs, despite the many different styles such as Chippendale, Sheraton, Hepplewhite, have this common structural feature. The mortise and tenon is the principal joint for these chairs, although in later and cheaper varieties, dowelling is used – normally two or three rods per joint. The seat and back can be wood, cane, rush or upholstery (the last, often of the drop-in type).

Upholstered frame chair This type is essentially an elaborate version of the two preceding types. The back legs extend through the seat in most cases, or are separate units. The main part of the chair, with the exception of the legs, is upholstered. As with the frame chair, mortise and tenon and dowelling are the standard joining methods.

Dismantling and rejoining chairs Loose joints are a common problem to all three types of chairs. Although time consuming in the long run it is worth the effort of dismantling the affected parts, cleaning out the joints and regluing. When only one member has come loose, it is tempting to try and force the others aside in order to get new glue into the joint. This may work if you happen to be restoring an antique chair and use the old cabinetmakers hide glue. This adhesive has the property of amalgamating with the existing glue and forming a satisfactory bond. Unfortunately in the majority of cases, forcing the chair apart puts considerable strain on otherwise sound parts. Ironically, it is the reglued joint that will hold the longest while the previously sound joints will come loose after a short time. As with all restoration work, take apart only what is absolutely

Below and bottom: Early nineteenth-century beechwood armchair with cane seat and simulated rosewood grain before and after restoration. Broken furniture usually looks more difficult to repair than it really is. This chair proved to be a simple job involving gluing the broken parts together before reassembly.

necessary. If you find that one joint of the seat rail has come loose and the rest of the chair is sound, the only other joint that will require opening will be its mate on the other side.

When all the joints are loose and a complete dismantling job is required it often saves time if you mark the joints with numbered tape before taking them apart. As some chairs can have as many as 18 separate components you can end up with an extremely frustrating jig-saw puzzle. Parts that look similar and interchangeable are in fact individually trimmed to fit their sockets and also affected by varying degrees of shrinkage. Another point to bear in mind before dismantling a chair is that in previous and misguided repair jobs, nails may have been driven clean through the joints. If you start knocking the chair apart without first noticing these and removing them, the joints will tear open and require a lengthy gluing job. Sometimes it is possible to punch the nail out from the other side. If this is not feasible, drill around the nail with a $\frac{1}{16}$-inch bit until a pair of point-nose pliers can be inserted and the nail withdrawn. The jagged hole left by the drilling can be cleaned up with a larger bit and filled at a later date with a wooden peg. A variety of hollow rotary rasps are available which are excellent for cutting the wood out from around the nail. Although the majority of joints can be loosened by hand, inevitably one or two will prove obstinate and refuse to come apart. Sometimes they can be tapped free with a wooden mallet or gently levered apart by using an inverted clamp.

A useful tip is to pick the chair up and tap the wood around the joint so that the shock effect is transferred to the joint until it falls out. If everything else fails, drill a small hole into the line of the joint and inject hot water with a syringe, so that the glue melts. If a modern resin-based glue has been used, a mixture of methylated spirits and paint stripper can be forced in. (You have to work fast if you are using a plastic syringe as the stripper will dissolve it.) A useful gadget for twisting turned chair rungs and legs free is the webbing clamp used by car mechanics for removing oil filters.

Before dealing with the individual problems associated with the three types of chairs there are a few points to remember. First, all joints should be thoroughly cleaned. Second, it often helps to 'dry join' the chair to ascertain that all the parts fit snugly and that all the holding clamps are of the right length. Finally while the glue is drying the whole chair should be clamped together on a level floor and left for the recommended setting time of the glue.

Stool or kitchen chairs The process for restoring the stool chair is very straightforward. It helps if you try to envisage the sequence in which the chair was made and then reverse the procedure to dismantle it. Firstly the legs should be removed from the seat and then, if necessary, the back. Remember to clean the glue from the sockets as well as from the pins on the stretchers and legs. Use a drill bit of the same dimension as the holes and twist it round by hand so that it gradually cuts and lifts out the old glue. Locking-jaw pliers can be clamped onto the bit if you require more torque.

Round joints in the stool chair often shrink with age. To get a really tight fit when required, a small saw cut should be made in the end of the stretcher, splat or leg. Into this insert a thin wedge of hardwood. As the part is glued and driven into its socket, the wedge is forced into the kerf to make a really tight fit.

When the dowel joints have snapped off in their housings they should be cut flush, drilled out and a false dowel inserted. Varying thicknesses of dowel rods can be purchased from most wood stores

Below: Replacement chair rungs can sometimes be fitted by gently prising open the joints with an inverted set of pole or sash clamps. This method saves dismantling the chair but can prove unsatisfactory since the pressure often weakens the remaining sound joints

Bottom: Turned parts joined by the socket method can often be freed by simply twisting and pulling the joints clear with a web strap.

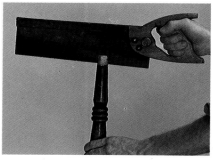

Top: Cleaning out a socket with a twist bit of the same dimension held with a pair of locking-jaw pliers. The bit will lift out the old glue without removing any wood.
Above: Cutting kerf lines into the top of a chair leg.
Right: Hardwood wedges inserted into the kerf lines. Once the leg is driven into its socket, wedges are forced into the cuts, causing the leg to expand slightly and take up the slack caused by shrinkage. The wedges should be cut as thin as possible to avoid splitting the leg open.

for this purpose. Once the rod is cut to the required length a thin channel should be run down the wood so that excess glue can escape.

On a kitchen chair screws are used only on the joint of the arm to back. Frequently you will find that these screws have rusted to such a degree that they have snapped off. Punch out the head of the screw from the upright and then withdraw the rest by making a nick across it with a file so that a screwdriver can be inserted. Broken screws that appear to be rusted solid can be freed by applying a soldering iron to the metal. This will burn off a thin layer of wood around the screw and thus enable it to be withdrawn. The new screw should be lightly oiled and then inserted so that the smooth shank passes the line of the joint. The countersunk hole can then be filled with a pellet of wood with matching vertical grain.

Since most of the parts of the stool chair are turned and canted at an angle away from the seat the best method of holding the chair during the setting of the glue is to use the Spanish windlass or tourniquet. This consists simply of winding a length of rope twice round the chair and twisting it up so that it tightens. Make sure that all the feet are level with the floor and that the angle of splay to the legs is uniform throughout.

One of the weak points of the stool chair is the rung or stretcher. These get broken by people using the chair as a ladder or by the sitter's foot being continually hooked over the rung. In some cases, particularly where the front stretcher has snapped in half, it is often possible to glue the crack and two sockets in place without dismantling the base completely. Both sides of the split should be cleaned off as well as the joints. A wire brush is ideal as it will remove any dirt or glue without affecting the profile of the jagged edges of the break. Sandpaper and steel wool are useless; all they do is blunt the join line. First glue the two halves of the rung into their respective sockets and then glue the crack. This middle section can be held in place by two hose clamps and then both the legs pulled together with a tourniquet.

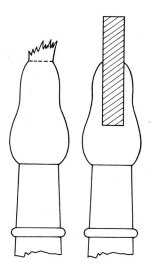

Far right: Where the extended pins to chair rungs have snapped off, the splintered part should be cut flush, a hole drilled and a piece of birch- or beech-rod dowel inserted to make a false peg.

Replacing a missing part to the stool chair, such as a leg or rung, is usually a long job if you do not have a lathe. Simple components can be shaped by hand with a surform tool and a profile gauge, but elaborate turnings should not be tackled, unless you are prepared for a long job. The Black and Decker lathe attachment will cope with most chair legs. With the aid of calipers and a cardboard template you will get a very accurate copy.

The wooden seat of the kitchen chair is usually made from hardwearing and nonsplitting timbers like elm, maple and ash. Occasionally, however, they do split and if it looks like the crack is going to open up even more, reverse the chair and make a mend from the underside of the seat. The best method is to close the crack up as tightly as possible with a sash clamp. With the clamp still in place, cut out a bow-tie shape from a piece of hardwood so that its grain will run across the crack. Mark round this shape with a craft knife and chisel out the 'grave' to a depth of $\frac{3}{8}$ of an inch. Once the bow-tie is glued in place it can be planed level with the seat. If the crack is really bad a metal brace can be screwed down either side of the crack instead of the bow tie. Ugly though this is, sometimes it is the only solution apart from cutting out the crack and laying a complete length of wood in.

Below and center: Split rungs can be clamped with two hose clamps. Providing the crack is thoroughly cleaned with a wire brush and the clamps left on overnight, the mend should hold without having to be pegged as well. Place thick card under the clamps to prevent bruising.

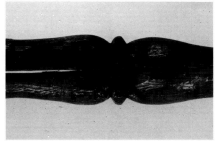

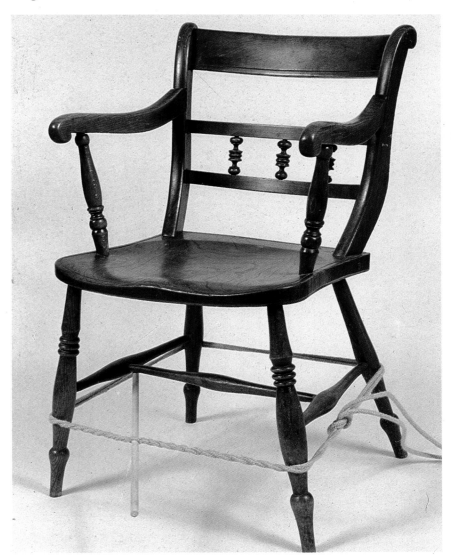

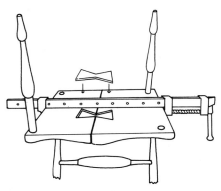

Above: Dropping a recessed wooden bow tie or butterfly cleat across the crack in a wooden seated chair. The repair should be made from the underside of the chair, with the grain of the cleat running at right angles to the crack.
Left: The tourniquet or Spanish windlass clamp is ideal for chairs with canted legs like this Windsor chair. Metal clamps tend to ride off when tightened.

Frame chair The frame chair category covers a larger and more varied group of seat furniture than the stool type. Each job has to be tackled according to individual circumstances. The back legs are usually curved while the front two can be a variety of shapes, from the elaborately carved cabriole leg to the reeded and concave saber. When clamping one of these chairs, blocks should be used to ensure that the joints are in line and that any carving, turning or angled corners will not be damaged by the hard steel edges of the clamp. A piece of softwood should be positioned over the top of the leg and the shape of the latter marked and cut out so that it fits exactly.

The main area of weakness in the frame chair is where the side skirts join into the uprights. The back usually pulls away from the seat where the stress is greatest. The standard join here is the mortise and tenon, though in later and cheaper varieties the finger joint and dowelling are sometimes used. With chairs that have an upholstered seat it is often possible to remove the webbing and coverings from the back alone without recourse to a complete recovering job at a later date. It helps to wedge a piece of scrap wood between the side

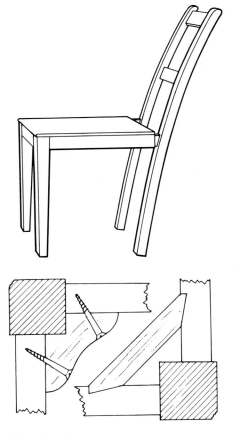

Top: The web clamp.
Center: Typical damage to a frame chair.
Above: Two types of corner brace.
Left: Painted Sheraton chair, circa 1800.
Shaped softening blocks prevent bruising while joints are reglued.

rails of the seat before pulling the two back joints free as this will maintain the shape of the seat and stop the webbing from pulling the rails out of line with the mortises in the back. All the loose upholstery, stuffing, webbing and canvas should be taped back and away from the gluing area so as to avoid marking them.

It is easier to rejoint a chair which has a drop-in seat that fits into a dado or rabbet running around the top of the seat rails. Once the seat is clear you will notice a system of corner braces. These keep the chair square and do away with the need for stretchers between the legs. When one of these corner struts works loose the leg will probably be insecure. Remove these before taking the chair apart, they are usually glued and screwed in place. Occasionally one of these blocks will be missing or badly split. Hold a piece of matching hardwood under the seat rails and mark off the two lines that form the gluing surfaces. Once these are cut, the remaining longest face can then be shaped to match the existing blocks. Always ensure that the grain of the wood runs parallel to the longest face. The new block should be glued in place and once the adhesive has set, can then be drilled and screwed for extra strength.

Repairing loose and worn joints A common problem associated with the mortise and tenon joint is that the tenon frequently becomes too small for its mortise owing to shrinkage and continuous use of the chair after the joints have worked loose. There are various methods of repairing the tenon, one of which is to pack the top and bottom of the worn joint so that all the faces are square and even. If the tenon still has its shape but is too small it can be made to fit tightly by blind wedging – make two narrow cuts and insert thin hardwood wedges into the kerf. As the tenon is glued and pulled home by the clamps, the wedges increase in width and thus ensure a tight fit. The mortise holes in the leg should be carefully pared to permit the wedged tenon to expand like a dovetail joint. This method makes the joint stronger than before but has to be done right first time! Once the the tenon has expanded it is extremely difficult to remove.

If severely attacked by woodworm, joints can snap off completely, leaving the tenon in the mortise. A false tenon must be inserted in the rail by chopping out a rebate so that a new piece of hardwood can be glued in place. Always work from the underside of the stretcher so that the mend is less conspicuous.

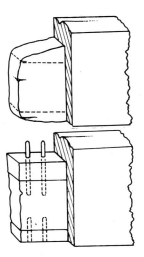

Right: The structure of any piece of furniture joined by the mortise and tenon depends on the joints being square and true. Worn tenons can be cut square and then packed back to size. Cocktail sticks can be used as miniature dowels for extra security.

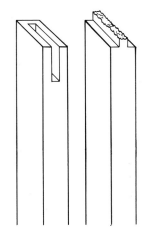

Below: Snapped tenons can be cut out from the underside of the apron or rail. A false tenon can be glued in place. Unless the chair is turned upside down, the repair is invisible.

Where dowelling has been used as the method of jointing in a frame chair and these have come loose or snapped off, remember to carefully clean out all the sockets before regluing. Beech- and birch-rod dowelling can be purchased in the two standard sizes used for most types of furniture – $\frac{1}{4}$ of an inch and $\frac{3}{8}$ of an inch.

Right: The front rail of a chair that has broken loose because of woodworm. To save taking the chair apart, make and test a false tenon (center and right). One half of it is then glued into the leg and, once dry, the rail can be dropped onto it and glued.

Frame chair backs Frame chairs with elaborate, shaped and carved backs often get damaged; usually the more fancy design the more likely will be the chance of breakages. Victorian-type Balloon-back chairs require a special system of clamping to replace their top cresting rails. The rails are usually fixed into the two uprights by dowels; because the curved shape of the wood inevitably results in end grain being exposed, they can snap across the weakest part of the wood. If the rail is simply loose, be careful how you rap it free of its dowels, too hard a blow will result in the wood snapping around the joint. Saw through the line of the joint with a fine hacksaw blade if the dowels will not come free. The dowels can then be drilled out from both sides with a drill bit half the size of the dowel. If you use a bit which is exactly the same size as the dowel it is very easy to wander off true and drill out part of the chair as well as the dowel. After drilling, collapse the rest of the peg with a fine chisel. Stubborn splinters left in the hole can be pulled out with point-nose pliers. Once both sides of the hole are clean you can drill deeper past the

Below: Typical area of damage to a late-nineteenth century Victorian balloon-back chair. The top cresting rail has snapped off, dowels and all.
Below right: Fix two small C-clamps (use softening blocks) on either side of the join. Once these are secured, two miniature tourniquets can be attached on the front and back. Tighten the front tourniquet and loosen the back or vice versa until the join line meets exactly. The old dowels should of course be drilled out and replaced beforehand. All that remains to be done to this chair is to remove the later plywood seat, restore the ebonized finish and recane.

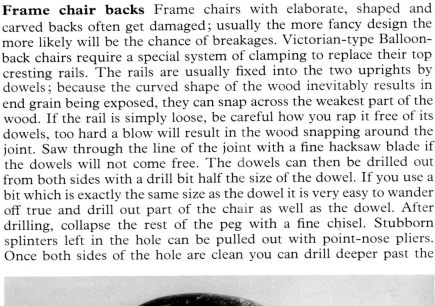
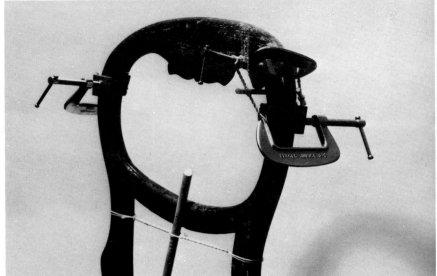

line of any cracks that might have occurred before cutting the replacement dowel to size. As with all dowel joints, chisel a groove down the length of the peg to allow excess glue and trapped air to escape.

The balloon type chair back is the most difficult of all varieties to clamp. Owing to the curved shape and slight rake, sash clamps will only pull the faces of the joint out of true. One good method is illustrated.

Clamp four pieces of scrap wood to either side of the join. Through either side of the clamp thread two tourniquets so that on tightening the joint will be pulled home. If the joint lifts slightly to one side loosen the tourniquet which is pulling too much and tighten its counter one until you have a perfect balance of pressure.

Chair stretchers If a chair rail breaks it is sometimes possible to mend the chair without having to make a complete new part. First remove both parts of the rail from their sockets, clean up the break if it has been previously glued and then clamp the pieces in alignment on a flat board. Make two angled saw cuts $1\frac{1}{2}$ inches either side of the break to a depth of half the stretcher. This area, which bridges the crack, can then be chiselled out and a matching piece of timber dropped and glued in to act as a splint. To ensure that the repair is unobtrusive the splice should face into the chair. If the stretchers are round in section, follow the procedure described in the section on stool chairs (*see page 74*).

Chair legs and associated problems Chairs that wobble and do not sit square on the floor can cause problems. Before taking any drastic measures, such as cutting the legs down to make them all the same length, make sure that discrepancies are not owing to a previous bad gluing job. Since the aim of restoration is to conserve as much as possible it is far better to pack the short leg and make it the right length rather than sawing off the three remaining good legs. Using a floor surface that is known to be true and level, it is easy to ascertain which leg or legs are short, either by using the eye or by using a spirit level. A $\frac{1}{2}$ inch difference can be made up by gluing and pegging a matching piece of wood to the bottom of the short leg.

A common break on the turned front legs of frame chairs is illustrated. The wood has snapped at its thinnest point and can be repaired by inserting a long dowel across the line of breakage. First drill well up

Below : Method of bridging a split in a chair stretcher. If the rest of the joints in the chair are sound, the two tenons should be glued into their mortises and then the crack and its splice clamped and glued. Once the adhesive has cured, the splice can be trimmed flush with a miniplane.

Right : Turned chair legs often break where the turning is thinnest. To repair the break, drill into the top part of the leg, then cut a section off with a fine tenon saw. Glue the cut-off section to the bottom of the leg. The hole drilled previously through this now acts as the guide for drilling down into the leg and the strengthening dowel will be exactly in line between the top and bottom. Place a thin piece of veneer between the two new meeting faces to make up the difference lost by the saw kerf.

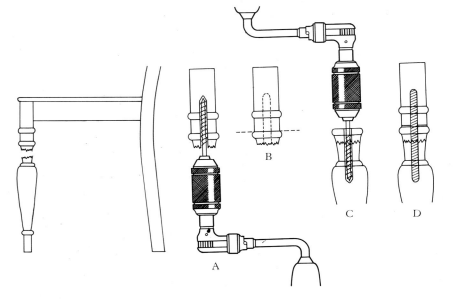

Above: Two methods of splicing new timber to a chair which has been cut down. The stepped and long splice avoid trying to glue end-grain timber. These additions are not required for wormed chair legs since these can often be saved by size or resin injection.

into the top part of the leg. Then cut the leg across at the line above the split. Use a fine tenon saw so as to avoid kerf wastage. Once this piece is free it can then be glued back onto its broken counterpart and allowed to set. As illustrated at C, you will now have a guide line for drilling down into the bottom part of the leg so that the two parts will be completely in line. Depending on the size of the leg $\frac{1}{2}$- or $\frac{3}{4}$-inch dowel should be used. If the tenon saw has produced a wide kerf you might find that the space lost in sawdust will have to be made up for with a thin piece of veneer. To test for correct thickness make a saw cut with the tenon saw in a piece of scrap wood. Various thickness of veneer can then be inserted to establish the correct width required for the spacer.

The old method of repairing a split or badly cracked square-sectioned leg was to screw the offending break together. This is a rather unsightly and unnecessary method of repair since a good gluing job is just as efficient providing the mend is effected before the edges of the crack become burred. Broken legs that have been left and knocked about for a period of time always prove difficult. To get a tight join, pegs instead of screws should be used. If you are a perfectionist the pegs can be countersunk and then pegged on top with a cut of wood whose grain runs across the end of the peg as opposed to down its length. Another alternative is to fit a piece of veneer into a small diamond-shaped recess cut around the peg so as to hide the end grain. This is often the best solution for valuable antique chairs as the repair is fairly inconspicuous.

Where legs have completely splintered, rotted and snapped off, either at the top or the bottom, the long splice joint has to be used. This is the most useful and common repair joint used in restoration since it does away with the difficulties of gluing end-grain wood and makes for an unobtrusive mend. A good deal of accuracy is required to get the two surfaces true and level as well as matching the grain direction. The new piece to be spliced on can be cut oversize so that subsequent trimming will ensure the continuous direction of the leg. Various types of splice joints can be employed for chair-leg repairs.

Upholstered chairs While areas of damage in most other types of chairs are readily apparent, the upholstered chair usually has to have its covering removed to show exactly what has come loose or has broken. Slight movement in the seat-to-back joints is frequently more serious than one would expect. The webbing and material will keep the whole structure together so that after a period of time and constant use loose joints become heavily rounded and worn. Illustrated is a typical beechwood framework on a nineteenth-century arm chair. One of the troublesome areas on this type of round-seated chair occurs at the point where the curved seat rail links into the back legs. Here, owing to the short-grained nature caused by the curved shape, joints frequently snap and have to be repaired with a false tenon that is pegged for extra strength.

Owing to innumerable re-coverings, many upholstered chair rails are shot to pieces by the hundreds of upholstery tacks that have been hammered into the wood. A temporary repair job can be effected by strengthening the wood with a bandage of hessian or fine canvas. If a thin glue solution is used (preferably hide glue) it will soak through the sponge-like timber and canvas to provide a good surface to tack to when it comes to rewebbing. Sometimes the inside edge will be so far gone that the spongy wood has to be rabbetted out and a new length of sound timber fitted in its place. A really thorough gluing job is needed here if you want to avoid using screws. The tremendous

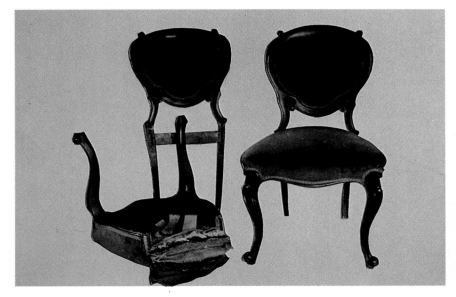

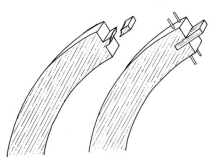

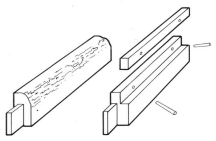

Above left: Typical damage to a Victorian balloon-back chair. A repair can be made without removing the upholstery by wedging a piece of scrap wood between the seat rails. This counters the pull of the webbing so that the tenons can be guided eàsily into the mortise. Once glued, remove the wood and retack the webbing.

Top: The tenons on the curved seat rail of upholstered pieces often break because end grain is exposed.

Center: Continuous reupholstery weakens the wood due to repeated nailing. A piece of burlap can be glued on underneath with cabinet glue.

Above: The rails of antique chairs can sometimes be saved by cutting out the heavily nailed section and replacing it with a sound piece of beech or other appropriate timber. This is glued and pegged at an angle.

Left: The framework of a Victorian chair. Note the curved rails, the use of beech for hidden parts, and mahogany for sections that will show once the chair is upholstered.

pull from the webbing once the chair has to bear a sitter's weight can easily rip the replacement out. Angled pegging at various points along and through the new wood will ensure a solid fixing. Seat rails and other beech or birchwood components in upholstered chairs provide an ideal breeding ground for the furniture beetle. Heavily attacked parts have to be replaced since they are an essential part of the structure of the chair – to try and upholster on top of them is asking for trouble.

Illustrated is the typical damage to an upholstered chair. Here the joinery takes the form of dowels. One of the front legs has snapped completely and the whole back of the chair has broken away from the seat. With a bit of patience and care the structure can be repaired without the need to reupholster. All the material and edge cord has pulled loose from around the affected parts and stitched or taped out

Left: A Victorian nursing chair. The upholstery is not original. The back seat rail joints and one of the front legs are broken.

Below: In order to get at the dowel joints for drilling and redowelling, the webbing had to be untacked and the stitchings to the welting unpicked.

of the way of the glue line. Once the canvas bottom and webbing are removed from the back and part of the side rail, the whole back can be lifted clear and the broken dowels drilled and chopped out. The whole structure is then repegged and reglued and, once firm, the webbing and covering is tacked back in place. One small problem arises in replacing the webbing as it will prove to be somewhat short so that it is rather difficult to get a good purchase on it. Two lengths of narrow scrap wood and a pair of locking-jaw pliers should provide adequate grip for pulling the webbing tight while the tacks are driven home with the free hand. This method will provide a couple more years of life from the existing upholstery of a chair that only has a few joints loose but it should never be employed on a chair with more serious forms of damage since a complete gluing job necessitates the removal of all the upholstery.

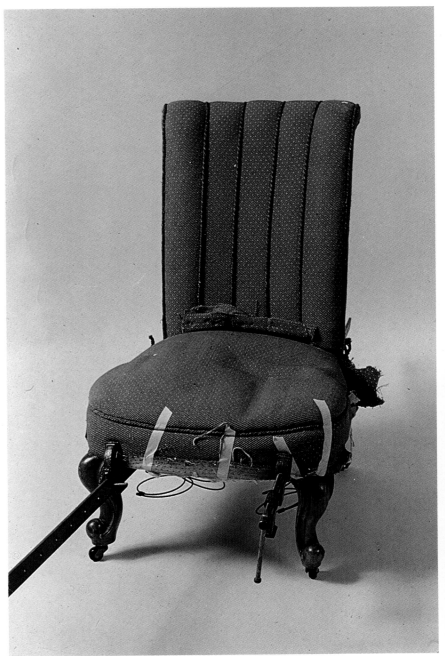

Left: All the loose upholstery material must be taped back out of the joint line to facilitate regluing. Place the chair on an even floor and clamp the joints with sash clamps. Release the clamps after 24 hours and retack and stitch the upholstery.

Below: The finished chair. The upholstery will last for a few years, but eventually it will have to be re-covered in the proper Victorian manner.

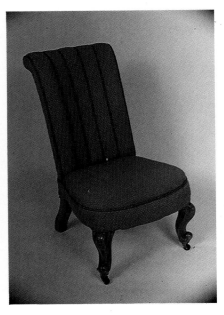

RESTORING TABLES

The table is one of the oldest and most common forms of furniture. Early types were simply a slab of wood resting on a trestle or X-frame base. Later, tables were supported by a leg at each corner and from this arrangement a great variety of styles have evolved. Before dealing with the methods of restoration it might be helpful to have a look at the six basic designs for this type of furniture. The smallest type is the pedestal or tripod table which consists in the first case of one or two columnar stems leading up from a platform base to link into the top. The tripod only has one stem and gets its name from the three-leg tripod arrangement at the base. The gate leg and its cousin the butterfly table are simply constructed around a central cage out of which two gates or slabs of wood are pulled on a pivot arrangement to support the fold-down leaves. A simplified version of the gate leg can be seen in the drop-leaf table, where the bottom stretcher which forms part of the gate shape is removed to provide more leg room.

Below: A late-17th century English fruitwood gate-leg table with bine-twist turnings.

Above: An English mahogany table, circa 1740.

Below: An antique oak tripod table with its top tilted back to show the platform, battens and locking plate. The underneath of the table top has been stained at some stage. Note the sheen, peculiar to the heavy use of stain.

The four-legged solid top table is perhaps the most common shape. It is composed of legs joined with stretchers or aprons and then screwed or pinned to the top. Here the whole piece is static and has no moving parts. A blend of the legged and drop-leaf variety produces the folding-top card or tea table where the arrangement is such that the top folds down and is supported by one or two of the back legs that pull out from the top of the base. The last standard shape is the trestle whose base is made up of two vertical slabs or X-frames secured by a centrally placed stretcher upon which the solid top rests.

There are of course hundreds of different variations of the above types but if you envisage any table without its frills and decorations it should fit into one of the six categories. For example, the country and farmhouse cricket table which only has three legs fixed into a circular top belongs to the legged bracket.

Many of the methods described in the chapter on chairs can be used in table restoration. Broken joints (usually mortise and tenon or the dowel type) and snapped legs can be fixed in much the same manner. Common sense is needed to choose the type of repair method which is going to be strong and unobtrusive. Problems confined to tables are broken mechanical joints and warping of large areas of solid wood. On modern types tops are usually constructed from laminated boards so you rarely come across the warpage and shrinkage problem. Warping in antique furniture is a more common occurrence that can lead to moveable joints jamming and putting considerable strain on other parts.

Extensive repairs should preferably be carried out with the base and top separated. This provides easy working and ensures that no further damage occurs. The common legged variety has its top secured to the apron by screws so often it is simply a matter of reversing the table on padded blocks or an old blanket and then removing these fixings. Rubbed glue blocks can either be steamed off or tapped away with a chisel and mallet. It can help to number the screws as they come out so that in the finishing stages of carpentry repairs they can be replaced in their respective holes. In past repairs different gauges and lengths often will have been used.

Pedestal and tripod tables The legs and tops of the pillar stem are the most susceptible areas in these types of tables. On the old tip-top tripod variety the central stem is secured into a platform which holds the top and at the base the three legs are joined in with long dovetails. In some cases the top is screwed to the platform but in the tip-top variety the whole top folds down for easy storage. Where the table top is composed of several solid wood boards these occasionally come unglued and the platform, with years of use, becomes loose from the central pillar. Turn the table upside down and remove the screws from the retaining battens or cleats. This will free the top so that it can be reglued. The arrangement for the tip top is illustrated; one of the battens has been removed to show the hinge peg around which the whole top folds down. On the antique types this hinge peg can become very worn and where the platform is loose anyway, it can prove easier to remove the whole of this block. Examination of the square of wood will show that the central pillar is secured by wedges driven into the end grain. These can be carefully chopped out with a chisel and once free the whole platform can be tapped away from the stem. Always fix the pillar stem in the vise to do this and wrap it in a thick cloth to prevent bruising. If you bash away at the wedges while the tripod is on the ground the legs will break off. With the platform

detached you can proceed to sorting out the worn hinge pegs by taking one of the battens and fitting it back onto the peg. If the gap is only minimal soak a thin strip of veneer and curl it round the peg to take up the slack. Where there is next to nothing left of the pegs the only solution is to cut out an $1\frac{1}{2}$-inch square length from the edge of the platform and refit a new piece of wood with new pegs carved from either end. It is important to peg and carefully glue this new section on as it will ultimately take the whole strain of the tip-up action.

When replacing the platform, be sure that it is fixed in the right position so that the hinge peg edge lies in line with the fork made by two of the tripod legs below. If you center just one of the legs, the top will jam when tilted. Once in position cut new hardwood wedges so that their end grain runs in an opposite direction to that of the square that appears through the platform. Tap these wedges home while ensuring that the platform is seated squarely on the stem.

Top: Unscrewing the retaining battens in order to free the top for regluing.
Above: One batten removed to show the pegs around which the top tilts. The elm platform has at some stage been repaired with a crudely fashioned nailed section.
Right: A 19th-century oak tripod table before restoration. Note how the platforms to these tables are always positioned so that when the top tilts it falls down into the space formed by the legs.

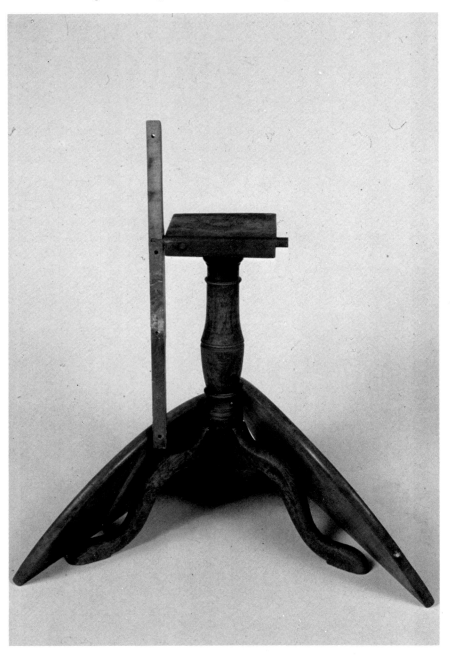

Regluing round tops As with all round wooden objects the problem lies in how to clamp them during gluing. All clamps tend to 'ride off' from such shapes when they are tightened up. The photograph shows a circular-topped tip-top table with its top in pieces and one of the battens left hanging on one of the pegs to the platform. To protect the edges in the repair of such a top and to ensure that the clamps do not slip, softwood softening blocks should be cut to shape (a coping saw will do this) and interposed between the hard metal edges of the clamp jaws.

Note that when the sash or pole clamps are tightened up the top tends to bow away from the clamp as would a piece of flexible plastic when squeezed between the forefinger and thumb. Large C-clamps can be fixed and tightened onto the metal bar in order to pull the top back in line (you might have to slacken the pole clamp at this stage). Do not overtighten these clamps otherwise the bar of the long clamp will bruise the wood. It is possible to insert a long piece of card between the clamp and the wood but this type of repair requires an octopus-like dexterity so the simpler you keep the operation the better. Once the top is clamped, all excess glue should be wiped off with a damp cloth. If you do not have a set of pole clamps then make yourself a set of folding wedges like those described in the tool section. Do not forget to place the shaped softening blocks in position before driving home your wedges. To counteract the bowing, nail a length of wood from one end of the folding wedges to the other. This will encase the top of the table in a kind of frame. Alternatively, simply place a heavy weight so that the top goes back to flat. Waxed paper between the table and the wood of the folding wedges prevents them sticking together. On small tables one clamp is usually sufficient but on the larger types two should be used. For extra security to the edges of the circle a long wooden peg can be drilled and driven into the top across the glue line as shown. Always get someone to help you on the larger tops and have all your clamps preset before starting to glue.

Top: Homemade device for clamping curved surfaces.
Above center: Using the device to provide a right angle for the sash.
Top left: Clamping in one operation. Pine softening blocks are used and C-clamps prevent bowing.
Above: The finished table.

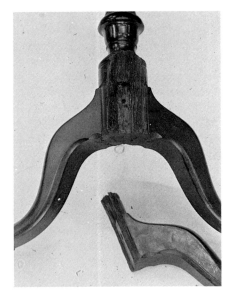

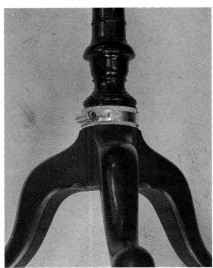

Loose and broken tripod legs Typical damage to the leg of a tripod is for the leg to rip away and take part of the pillar with it. The best method of repair is to try and separate and free the broken parts of the stem from the leg, reglue them to the pillar and then return the leg to its dovetail housing. Sometimes this is very difficult to do without causing further damage to the splintered parts and a less satisfactory solution can be achieved by using a hose clamp to hold the leg back in place while the glue dries. This, unfortunately, will only apply pressure to the top of the break line so, with your base inverted in the vise, pull the toe end of the leg in toward the stem by using a Spanish windlass. Nail a large nail into the workbench to act as the fixing for the end of the windlass. Always ensure that the pull of the windlass is in line with the leg, otherwise the leg will rip out at an angle. On some types of tripods, because of this notoriously weak area, metal straps are fixed underneath the legs for extra strength. These have to be removed when the legs have come loose so that the dovetail joint can be pulled free. Another quick repair job in the past was to screw through the legs into the stem. This is a useless and unsightly method of repair and such screws should be removed and their holes plugged with end-grain timber. Once the glue is set, such pegs can be cut flush and if you make them with the grain running across the peg as opposed to down it such a repair will match in a better fashion. Although the metal straps that can be found on antique pieces might not be original, unusually in restoration, such metal strappings should be replaced. They are unobtrusive once the table is returned to the upright position. Occasionally when all three legs have to be removed to effect a decent repair, drill a neat hole with a $\frac{1}{16}$-inch bit down the line of the join and inject the appropriate solvent down the glue line. Use hot water in the case of antique table bases where old cabinetmaker's glue had been used. As the glue softens the legs can be tapped free or simply pulled out. Sometimes you have to work the leg back and forward in the joint once you have reached the first 'give' in the bonding. With the legs free it is often easier to splice on missing feet and sort out cracks and the like. Obviously if the whole table is sound then such an operation is unnecessary and repairs to just one of the feet should be carried

Top left: A broken tripod leg.
Center left: Hose clamp in action.
Far left: Old metal bracing straps.
Left: Repegging a bad repair.
Above: Injecting a solvent to free the legs for further repairs to the stem.

out with the whole piece intact. Using a complete leg as the pattern you can gauge the shape of the missing parts. It is essential to cut the joint at an angle so as to avoid end grain, which never glues properly, and to provide a larger gluing surface. In all similar scarf repairs, always cut your replacement oversize so that any slight discrepancies can be sorted out when it comes to the carving and shaping stages. It is possible to get a perfectly flat meeting surface by simply buying a rigid circular sander for your motorized drill and fix the two either into a drill stand or a vise. Such metal disks are very cheap and if you do not own a drill already it is definitely worthwhile getting one. As with many replacements in restoration, take your parts to the sander as opposed to taking the machine to the wood.

Return the legs to the stem after repairs to test the fit before gluing. This is the point to check for looseness and to pack out with veneer any gaps. The legs should tap home easily but should not be too loose. If you have to force them then you have either got the leg in the wrong socket or you will have packed out too much.

1. A sound leg is used as a pattern to gauge the shape of the replacement.
2. A new section is spliced onto a mahogany leg.
3. The replacement is shaped with a spokeshave.
4. The mend awaiting staining after final finishing with the cabinet scraper.
5. So much wood is cut out of tripod stem bases that inevitably they split open down one of the long dovetail recesses. After repairs to the stem, the legs are tested in a dry run to check for firm jointing.

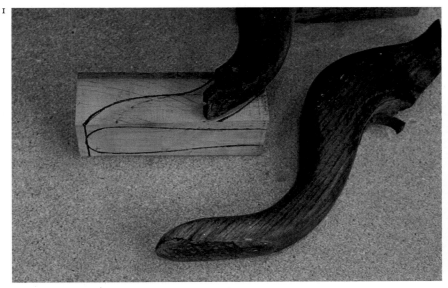

1

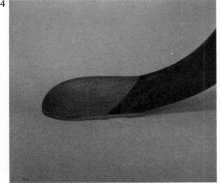

4

2

3

5

Table stems and circular leg repairs The restoration of the Cuban mahogany wine table with fixed top illustrated is probably beyond the beginner's capabilities but it does show the stepped method of repair which can be used on legs and stems. Also it shows what can be done with the cheap lathe attachment. A discourse on how to use a lathe would be too great a digression and those interested should take up lessons in the subject before tackling furniture. It is easy once you have got the hang of the process. Illustrated is a table with the bad repair to the top removed and the repair screws still in place. Unfortunately large pieces of Cuban mahogany are like gold dust so a piece of the paler colored Honduran mahogany was substituted. This was cut from a Victorian piano leg found in a junk shop. Once the basic square shape was spliced on and turned, the wood was chemically darkened to match with bichromate of potash and then polished. The turning was stopped just short of the original surface and finished off by hand, this way none of the original patination was destroyed. This restoration job was a long and involved process as the legs had to be removed to get the pillar onto the lathe but it was worth the time spent. You can use the stepped method of repair for badly cracked legs to tables and on the simpler types which do not have fancy ring turnings, a lathe is not essential as much of the shaping can be done with the surform and sandpaper.

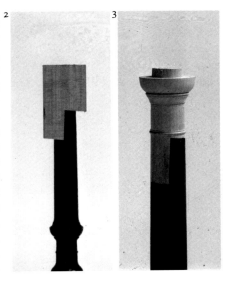

1. A Cuban mahogany tripod table, circa 1780, awaiting restoration. A bad repair had been made to top of the stem in pine. The repair screws were removed by using a locking-jaw pliers on one side and a screwdriver on the other.
2. A square of Honduras mahogany was then glued on.
3. The legs were freed by the injection method, and then the stem and its block were mounted on the lathe and turned to match the overall pattern. The turning was stopped a fraction short, to avoid cutting into the original wood, and finished off by hand.
4. The finished table.

Restoring working parts to drop-leaf and fold-over topped tables On most tables where a good-quality hardwood has been used for the top, leaves and legs, working parts and hidden frame constructions are usually made up from the cheaper woods such as pine, beech and elm. The woodworm has a field day with such woods so as well as having worn mechanical joints, the underparts are likely to be thoroughly wormed. Illustrated is a drop-leaf pedestal table whose flaps are supported on pull-out flippers as opposed to the gate arrangement. The top has been removed and the detail shows how one of the flippers has broken away due to heavy worm attack. Such a mechanical joint, called a knuckle or working-finger joint, is easy to replace. They vary in size, shape and arrangement from table to table but, as in all restoration work, it is simply a matter of copying one of the remaining sound parts. If the whole lot is rotten as was the case here, it can be a great help to try and remove one of the parts intact. Do not rip the whole lot to pieces as you will have no pattern to work from. Cut a knuckle and use a 4-inch nail in place of the missing pin. The fingers have to be cut with total precision so use a mortise gauge to mark out the lines. Once finished, the action should be tight and fairly stiff. Use a coping saw to cut out the waste wood between the teeth once you have cut the lines down with the backsaw or dovetail type. Clean and square up with a sharp chisel. On the existing flippers you will notice that the back has been chamfered away so that when a person reaches under the table they can get their hand behind the back to pull the flipper out. Cut this recessed chamfer with the coping saw before fixing the two parts together. Now the back edges of the teeth have to be chamfered and the spaces between chiselled out in a semicircle – it is best to copy the existing pattern on your table. The tricky part is to drill a dead vertical line down through the teeth in order to fit the pin. Use a long bit and with the brace, drill right down the center of the teeth or interlocking fingers. It helps to have someone to tell you whether you are drilling at the right angle, or to use one of the modern dowelling jig attachments.

1. A 19th-century mahogany drop-leaf pedestal on platform base. The top has been removed in order to replace the flippers.
2. A detail of the badly wormed flipper.
3. Testing the new flipper to see that the knuckle is tight.
4. A modern nail is used in place of the missing pin. Once the knuckle has been drilled through, the nail is dropped in place and the excess head and point cut off with a hacksaw.

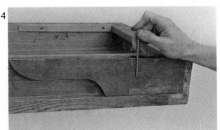

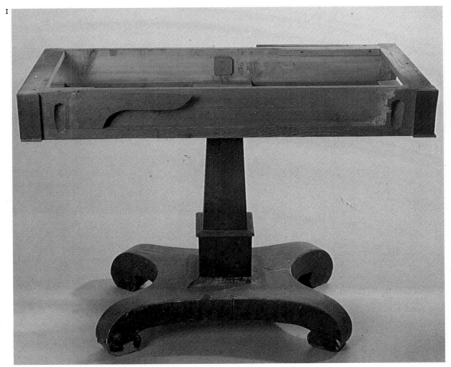

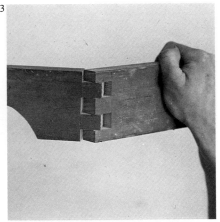

In the case of this table the static part of the flipper was glued and nailed to the side frames. Note that in what is left of the flipper a recess has been cut, through which the screw is fed to hold the top. This has to be copied in the new flipper. The completed table can be seen with one of the leaves up and supported by the flippers.

Left: The finished table, with one of the leaves supported on the new flippers.

Bottom left: Folding-top table with one half of the top removed. The swing leg has fallen off owing to woodworm.
Below: The original wormed section is used as a guide for cutting a new piece in elm.
Bottom: Using the original as a guide for cutting on a band saw.

Similar mechanical joints can be seen in the fold-over tea table illustrated. One half of the top has been removed and the gate and its leg taken away for repair. The elmwood apron and swing-out part to the leg was totally rotten with worm and while it might have been restorable if it had been a piece of surface timber, as a structural component and a working part it had to be replaced. Using the rotten part as a guide, along with measuring where the leg would stop on the table itself, a new piece of elm was cut to shape to fit in the leg at one end and to provide the knuckle joint at the other. The rotten part is used to make the pattern for the knuckle. Once the leg and its gate were glued together and tested, the next stage was to chisel away the rotten wood on the other side. All that remains to be done is to paint the new replacements with milk paint and refix the other half of the top. Such a swing-gate action is standard for most types of folding tops and drop-leaf tables. On the better examples both the

legs swing out from the back. Where the knuckle joints have simply worn down and the leg leans drunkenly at an angle when pulled out, simply put hardwood spacers between the knuckles. You might have to take the top off and pull the pin from the knuckle to do this but it is worth doing as the table will only get worse.

Above: The replacement can now act as the guide for the other half of the knuckle. The original but badly wormed section is chiselled clear. As these are working joints, conservation is very difficult.
Left: The old and the new. The 'milk paint' finish is simulated with pigment colors, with water as the base and cabinet glue as the binder.

Sagging drop leaves When drop leaves are extended and supported by the legs they can hang down at a slight angle from the horizontal. This is because the top of the swing gates becomes worn with the constant friction against the underside of the leaves. Have a look under the table and you will see heavy score marks in a quarter circle. Simply clamp a stout piece of timber right across the whole top so that the leaves and central portion are flat and in line. If you now have another look under the table you will be able to see the tapering gap between the top of the gate and the top. Cut a length of matching timber and glue and peg it in place to take up the gap. Do not use nails as these will eventually cut through into the underside of the top as the wood wears down. The taper to your piece of packing can be produced by holding the part against the rigid circular sander. Once the glue has set, release the clamps and the top should stay flat.

Splits in table tops and leaves Inevitably when large areas of solid wood are used in furniture, splits occur. These usually follow the grain and 'run out' halfway down the board. Closing up the gap with a sash clamp and glue rarely works on the wider cracks. As soon as the pressure from the clamp is released the crack springs open once more. The best method is to gently close up the gap with the clamps and then to let a butterfly cleat into the underside of the table where it will not be noticed. On p 88 is the recess for one of these cleats already cut and interestingly it shows the ugly and unnecessary batten-type support, which should be avoided if possible. With the cleat in place (on a long crack you might need two) the crack can now be packed with a taper of thick veneer of the same wood as the table. Once the glue has set, carefully pare back the veneer until it is level with the table and ready for staining and matching in. It is essential that both sides of the crack are level with each other so throughout the operation keep checking the edge at eye level. For extra security and to maintain the level, the edge can be pegged through at an angle across the crack.

Rejointing boards to square table tops Some of the mahogany trees that were felled in the eighteenth century must have been

Below and bottom: Dropping a sliver of mahogany veneer into a crack. The taper to the veneer is produced by pulling the wood over a plane blade. Once glued in place, the veneer is carefully levelled until flush with the top.

enormous. Solid unjointed planks from antique dining tables can measure up to 4 feet in width. Such pieces usually belong to the top end of the market and the more humble table top is frequently composed of several boards jointed together to make up the necessary width. Problems can occur with these types in that while wood rarely shrinks along the grain, large gaps will appear between the planks as the wood shrinks across the grain.

Removing the top and closing up the gap on drop-leaf varieties can lead to problems. The top will be smaller in width so that when it is replaced the leaves will jam against the base of the table and stick out at a slight angle rather than falling vertically flush with the sides, so it is always best to first check how much width you are going to lose and whether it will affect the leaves. When the gap is really wide a fillet of matching wood will have to be dropped in instead. The success of this operation depends on having the right timber in your workshop. Filling the gap with a shellac stick is never really satisfactory so do not use it on valuable tables.

On the single-topped type of legged table even if the top is reduced in size it will not affect the overall appearance. If the meeting surfaces between the boards are out of line make up a shooting board as described in the tool section and plane away the discrepancies. Then the boards can be clamped together with the folding-wedge method. Some people like to dowel at the same time but this is not really necessary if your edges are perfect and you do a good glue job. As usual, clean off the glue as it is squeezed out by the pressure and make sure that the meeting edges are level. When you replace the top on the base it can help to plug all the original screw holes, center the table top, and drill a set of new ones, using the holes in the apron or frame as a guide.

Above: A 1930s oak gate-leg table. The gate has broken loose from the frame.

Gate-leg tables A common occurrence in the gate-leg and butterfly type of table is for the pins or dowels (which act as the pivot for the whole square frame of the gate) to break or become worn. The gate is secured between the top and bottom stretchers of the central part of the table. Without dismantling the whole table to get the gate back in place with its new pegs fitted, it is possible to remove the top and extend the receiving sockets right through the rails. With the leg in place and its socket smeared with a light coating of glue, the new peg can be inserted through the stretcher so that it only adheres to the socket in the leg and not the top. Now the table can be turned upside down and the same process carried out with the bottom socket. Before you do this, make sure that glue in the top socket has gelled, otherwise it will run out and stick the leg to the stretcher. A blob of glue can now be inserted into the bottom sockets so that it misses the sides of the stretcher but drops into the leg. If the pegs are cut to one-third the depth of the stretcher, two smaller lengths of pegging can be lightly glued in place to fill the holes.

The rule joint on the leaf of the table can also cause problems. In damp conditions the top will expand and cause this type of working joint to jam. An immediate solution is to move the hinge slightly out from its fixing in the central part of the table so that the joint clears when the top is erected. All the old screw holes have to be replugged, and it sometimes works on the cruder types of rule joints. However, in most cases it is essential that the pivoting part of the hinge lies directly under the line where the leaf meets and closes up on the table top. Frequently the only solution is to stand the table in a dry and fairly warm room so that the wood shrinks back to its original size.

Warping Warping in table tops can be tricky and frequently there

is not a satisfactory solution. In antique furniture minor warps are acceptable, so unless they are really bad it is best to leave well alone. Bear in mind that wood expands when wet and shrinks when dry and that this movement always occurs across the grain and rarely down it. A length of fairly wide timber whose two surfaces are subjected to damp conditions on one side and dry on the other will naturally warp toward the dry side, due to the expansion of the wet side. Imagine that you are viewing the table tops from the top throughout this section so there is no confusion over the terms concave and convex warping. The former is where the top bows downward and away from you so that the edges of the table are higher than the center and the latter is where the opposite occurs and you get a dome shape.

Until the mid-1700s and even later few craftsmen realized that to protect wood completely from atmospheric conditions both sides of the boards had to be sealed. In the majority of cases only the visible and external parts were polished while underparts and inner surfaces were left. Hence, the unfinished parts reacted and moved according to conditions of damp or dryness while the outside and top surfaces were relatively unaffected. On the cheaper types of furniture plain-sawn planks are used instead of the more expensive quarter- or radially-sawn types which reduces warping to a minimum and shrinkage only occurs in the thickness of the board and not the width. The plain-sawn method causes shrinkage in the width of the board and the heartwood side usually shrinks less rapidly than the sapwood side, causing warping. If you examine the end grain of your top you will be able to see which method of sawing has been used. In the radial- or quarter-sawn method the growth rings run at a right angle to the surface of the board while in the other method they run almost parallel with the surface.

Warps in solid wooden tops

One/The concave warp: It is possible to redress the balance in the board by soaking the shrunken side (that is the top surface in these cases) with water. Remove the whole top from the table and cover the concave side with a wet cloth or heavily dampened blotting paper. In some cases you will have to remove the finish to allow the water to penetrate. It is essential that the whole top is covered in a uniform fashion otherwise the water will leave ugly marks in the wood. I have a sheet of 3×4 feet blockboard which has one side covered in plastic sheeting. This is placed on top of the table top and clamped down. Thick battens provide uniform pressure between the clamps and the table top and as each of the six clamps is tightened down they gradually force the warp flat against the blockboard. Initially little pressure is used but as the wood begins to absorb the moisture the clamps are tightened progressively, until after a two-hour period or so the warp disappears. If you do not have a piece of blockboard or enough C-clamps, then the best method is to use 6 battens through which large nuts and bolts are screwed and fixed. These work just as well but the disadvantage here is that without the blockboard to distribute the pressure, water is forced out of the cloth in greater quantities directly under the battens. Frequently three large black striped watermarks are left in the surface when you remove the battens. Water that is left between an object and a table top penetrates far deeper into the wood than does a pool left on the surface. Hence the problem with ring marks left by drinking glasses. The blockboard method distributes the water into the wood in an even fashion so that even if you get a slight darkening effect at least it is uniform.

This method works on thin table tops but on 90 percent of the

Below: Refixing the gate without taking the frame apart.

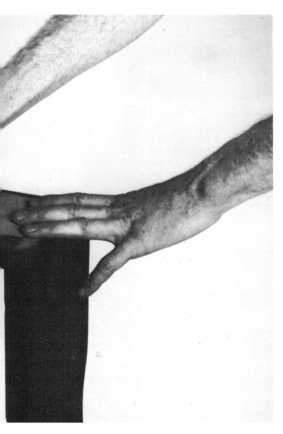

useful to have a second pair of hands when you do this rather tricky job – someone to feed one side of the chest into the base while you return the other side. Once the piece is clamped with pole clamps or a tourniquet, measure from the top left-hand corner of the chest to the bottom right-hand corner, starting and finishing your measuring in the corners of the empty drawer housings. Now check that the measurements are equal with the imaginary line drawn from the top right to bottom left. If your measurements are not equal, loosen your clamps and adjust the carcass, and retighten. This will ensure a perfect 'square' to the chest.

Repairs to feet and underparts Once your carcass is sound, check underneath to see if all the feet are secure. Older types of chests have a simple arrangement for fixing the bracket feet and skirts to the base. The section on joints in furniture shows how a system of rubbed glue blocks is used to lock the underparts together. When the feet are loose, first remove the glue blocks, clean out the blocks and then replace them. Most glue blocks can be tapped free with a chisel, the feet repaired and the blocks replaced. This is another example of the quality of old cabinetmaker's glue. First heat up the back of the skirt and the block, apply the glue and then rub the block backward and forward – they will set after two or three pushes backward and forward. No clamps are needed provided the two faces are clean and warm before you glue them. Use a blowtorch to warm the wood, running it in a series of rapid passes across the wood – do not hold the blowtorch on one spot or you will scorch the wood. Never use a blowtorch near polished, patinated or finished surfaces.

If a section of a bracket foot is missing you can make a cardboard template from an existing foot and cut out a new one with a coping saw. If all the feet are missing you should look through an illustrated book on furniture history for a pattern to copy which is in keeping with the carcass. Round holes in the base of the carcass of the antique teak-wood miniature box of drawers illustrated were the only clues that the piece originally had bun feet. The shape of the ebony inlay in the drawer fronts was taken as a pattern for replacement bun feet which were turned on the lathe from pearwood. Then the feet were ebonized (*see* finishes) and fitted into the existing sockets.

Problems with drawers Wear and tear in drawers is particularly noticeable when the drawer front sits back from the face of the chest of drawers and the drawer no longer runs smoothly. In older pieces the runners on the bottom of the drawer and inside the chest get very worn, particularly toward the back. Where a drawer has been badly worn you can plane away the uneven section without interfering with the drawer bottom. On flat-bottomed drawers the wear is usually even and you are unlikely to come across this sort of problem. Cut a new piece of wood, tapered at one end and glue it into position on the newly planed edge of the drawer. It is essential to clamp the wood while the glue sets. Do not nail the wood – the metal head will eventually appear at the surface and wear down the runner again. Cut the new tapered piece of wood overlarge, when the glue has set plane it down to size so the drawer runs smoothly.

Worn drawer runners The drawer runner is the projecting support inside the chest on which the drawer sits. If the bottom of the drawer is worn (as described above) there will usually be some damage to the carcass runner too. If the wear is particularly bad on a veneered piece there is a danger that pieces of veneer will be torn away from the drawer divide as the drawer is pulled and pushed out of alignment. Before replacing the veneer, damaged parts of the

WOODWORM, BAMBOO and BENTWOOD

Before dealing with badly wormed wood, affected parts should be injected with a proprietary fluid such as Cuprinol or Rentokill. Find a hole every inch and inject it with the solution. On pieces which do not have an immaculate finish the solution can be brushed on as well. Leave the piece for about a week to allow it to dry out.

One of the first lessons in all cabinetmaking schools is to make all joints as neatly as possible and to finish off all surfaces perfectly. The furniture beetle has to lay its eggs in a crack or splits in order for them to survive and hatch into grubs. The beetle itself has no boring device for drilling a hole into the wood; consequently when it alights on a well-made piece of wood and cannot find a recess between joints, it leaves in search of something more suitable. Unfortunately, with time, furniture develops a crack here and there, and unfinished interior surfaces become ideal breeding grounds for the furniture beetle. It is the grubs which do the damage; they eat their way through the wood to the surface leaving small piles of dust behind them. Badly wormed legs and feet on older pieces can become structurally unsound and while in the past such components were replaced, the restorer's wish to conserve as much of the original as possible has resulted in two methods of strengthening sponged timber. The method employed about 20 years ago used size to strengthen a badly infected leg. By size is meant the old fashioned variety obtainable from chemists and specialist paint shops, not modern wallpaper adhesive. It comes in a concentrated powder form and is made in the same way as cabinet glue. Parings of old leather, hoofs and parchment are boiled and then dried to produce the powder. The leg of the table can be strengthened as follows: Boil the size with water in a double glue pot. While the size is heating up turn the piece upside down and form a well from card or modelling clay round the damaged leg. When the size is very hot and runny (but not boiling) pour it in – about a teacupful of liquid size should be enough. Let the size soak into the wood – this will take about 24 hours.

The alternative and more modern method uses the latest developments in plastics and resins. Buy a two-part resin casting solution from the local craft shop which is liquid enough when mixed to be injected into the wood through a hypodermic syringe. Epoxy-resin glues and car body-resin kits are too thick for this job, and avoid the brittle simulated-glass compounds. Gently tap the affected leg until all the woodworm dust has fallen out of the holes and the passages are clear. When you are sure all the dust is out, start injecting every hole with resin. As the resin runs down the passages it will start to appear out of the side holes – these should be taped up to force the resin further down the leg and not out of the sides.

Bamboo repairs In the Far East, where bamboo furniture was used for centuries, it was beautifully made with pegs and without glue. However, the bamboo furniture made in nineteenth-century Europe was simply made, and held together with nails. By the twentieth century, bamboo was an immensely popular cheap type of furniture, often combined with Japanned panels or areas of grass matting.

The most likely problem with bamboo is that after a while it becomes rickety. The hollow center of the bamboo is usually plugged with a piece of softwood at places where joints have to be made. This

Below: Strengthening the wormed feet of a mid-17th century oak table base. This size contains an antifungi agent.
Bottom: A late-19th century bamboo cabinet with Japanned top and doors.

enables those dreadful long pins to be driven through the bamboo and fixed to something solid. Taking bamboo furniture apart in order to replace a badly smashed section or to rejoin it can send you up the wall. Each joint is usually fixed by three pins driven in in totally opposite directions and frequently the only solution is to carefully rock the piece backward and forward to force these out so you can grip the ends with a pair of point nose pliers. Unfortunately, most of the time the pin has rusted solid into the softwood plug and all that happens is that the pin cracks the bamboo. Better quality furniture is jointed by the plug method. You will require bends on the legs of bamboo cabinets where they sweep out at the bottom. Buy a new piece of bamboo or salvage another section from a wreck, heat the section over a blowtorch and press the area until it bends. Hot water can also be used to make the material pliable but this tends to destroy the natural shine. Old bamboo does not bend quite as well as green bamboo. The outer casing of bamboo will resist most kinds of glue. Epoxy resins sometimes stick to the shiny surface and act as a packing to the original and badly cut joints. By filing off the meeting surfaces with a rasp, a good joint can be made sometimes with cabinet glue. Always bore holes with a $\frac{1}{16}$-inch bit into your new sections so that the nails do not split the bamboo.

Cracks in legs and lengths can be fixed by injecting one of the new thin liquid glues such as the 'miracle' or 'super' glues. Fill the crack with glue and squeeze the sides together. Be careful when working with these glues – it is very easy to find yourself stuck to the piece.

Stripping and polishing bamboo Bamboo is not easy to stain and there is a danger that the stain will go blotchy. Modern bamboo furniture is colored with a mixture of French polish and stain. You can patch areas with a fine sable brush and a mixture of spirit aniline dye and French polish. Oak and walnut spirit stains with a dash of yellow will produce the right tone. If you feel the piece has to be stripped, use fine steel wool and methylated spirits and avoid getting it near any inset Japanned panels.

Bentwood furniture Much of this type of furniture dates from the early nineteenth century and although the Windsor chair can be classed as bentwood, here we are dealing with the variety associated with makers like Michael Thonet. Most bentwood furniture in this bracket is made from birch-rod strips. The rods are steamed into shape around a series of jigs by heat and pressure.

Likely areas of damage are where the curve or bends are sharpest, usually on the back of the chair where the rod is taken right over and back down to form the leg. Splits occur in the same manner as those produced by bending a green twig from a tree. The twig cracks in a 'run' down the length without actually coming apart. Simple gluing and clamping rarely proves to be a good repair because, once the piece has cracked, forces are released in the wood which require cunning as opposed to brute force to rectify.

Without spending hours in a steamed-up bathroom trying to make the wood more flexible, the split can be repaired by creating the same conditions under which the chair was originally made. By making a steam gun you can localize pressure and heat to the area of repair. Use a small can with a removeable lid. Punch a hole in the lid and insert a 3-inch length of $\frac{1}{2}$-inch rubber hose (garages stock the black vulcanized variety). Place the can on a low heat; after a while steam should issue out of the end of the hose.

First of all, remove the damaged back from the chair; most types of bentwood are bolted to the seat. Once free, strip about 4 inches of the

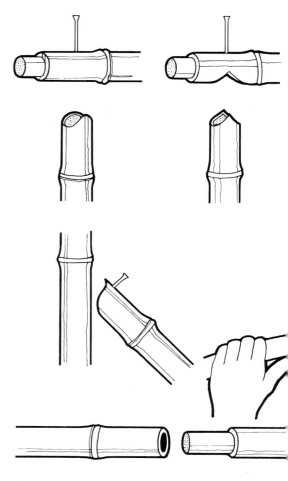

Above: Various bamboo joints. Curves to replacements can be made as illustrated. The sharp 'kick' to the legs of the cabinet on the preceding page was made by pressing the bamboo against a metal rod during the heating.

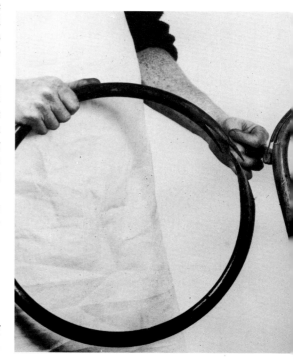

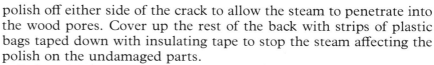

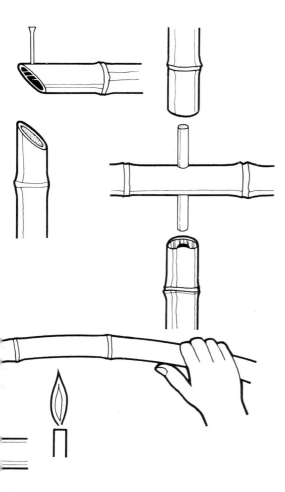

polish off either side of the crack to allow the steam to penetrate into the wood pores. Cover up the rest of the back with strips of plastic bags taped down with insulating tape to stop the steam affecting the polish on the undamaged parts.

Before starting to steam the split, it is essential to secure a piece of waterproof tape around the area where the crack starts to open out. On top of the tape a hose clamp should be tightly fixed. This will prevent the crack running down the wood completely when you start to steam.

Put two loose hose clamps over the end of the leg and run them up to the area of the crack, leaving them hanging free for the moment. Now, with your hands protected by thick rubber gloves, aim your steam nozzle at the crack. Keep this localized heat and pressure up until the wood becomes flexible (alternating between the steam gun and a blow torch will sometimes speed up the process). As the wood becomes pliable stop the steam and start to position and tighten up the hose clamps. I like to have a premeasured strip of thick but flexible plastic sheeting placed between the wood and the clamps to prevent bruising. As you continue steaming gradually tighten up the clamps until the crack meets perfectly. Now leave the piece clamped for at least 24 hours so that the wood dries out thoroughly. Once you release the clamps you will notice that the split only opens slightly. Feed some strong waterproof resorcinol glue into the crack, making sure that it penetrates right to the back of the crack. Now tighten the clamps once more and leave the glue to set, making sure to wipe off the excess as it is squeezed out. For extra security you can also pin the cracks in four places with rods. As you return the legs to the base you will notice that the gap between them will be greater than before. Fix one leg loosely in place and then gently bend the other until you can feed the bolt through the leg hole and the seat. Tighten up and proceed to refinish the top part of the rail. Due to the steaming, the area around the crack will have furred up slightly into a kind of driftwood finish. Lightly sand the fur off and then stain and polish to match the rest of the chair.

Below left : The natural and damaged break to be found on bentwood. The former is where the original joint has opened.
Below : Use the steam gun from all angles while tightening up the hose clamps.

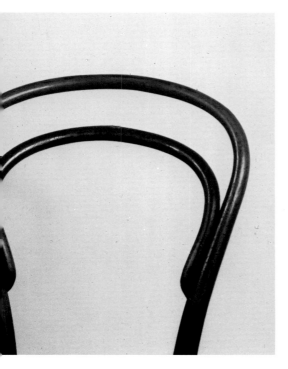

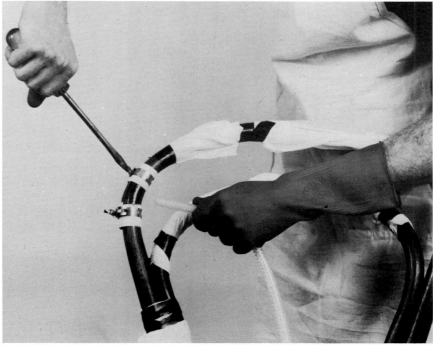

FURNITURE HARDWARE and METAL REPAIRS

In this section we shall be dealing with furniture metalwork such as handles, locks hinges and brass inlay. Many simple jobs can be tackled with a limited amount of tools and a degree of ingenuity, but badly damaged handles that form part of an original set on antique furniture should be removed and taken to the expert. Such repairs are usually very expensive.

Tools Most of these have been mentioned already in the chapter on tools – you will need a hacksaw, various metal files, a blowtorch, pliers, a small metal-headed hammer, a knife and, last, a vise with metal-faced jaws.

Materials You will need brass polish, glass-fiber resin and hardener (the sort used for filling dents in cars), mineral and penetrating oil, modelling clay, two-part epoxy-resin adhesive and a small selection of metal-based paints (bronze-dust and brass-colored types).

Cleaning metal handles The easiest job is cleaning up tarnished handles and so on. I prefer simply to wipe them over with a dry cloth but there is a certain amount of disagreement in the antique trade about whether brass pulls and handles should be highly polished or left as found. The surface of metals like iron, bronze and brass go through a chemical change when exposed to the elements in the air, which forms a dull coating of oxide. When this is removed with brass polish, a minute layer of the metal is taken away so that over the years the handles and pulls get worn away. Naturally cleaned handles add to the overall effect on modern pieces of furniture, but on the antique piece I would not advocate too much cleaning. Original handles are as much a part of a piece of furniture as the woods and finish.

Missing handles and back plates A missing handle from a chest of drawers can frequently be replaced with a modern copy bought from a hardware store or from a mail-order firm specializing in antique reproductions. Chippendale- and Empire-style handles, although varying slightly, follow basic patterns. Slight discrepancies in shape are not too noticeable as long as you do not drill fresh holes in your chest front in order to fit them.

Back plates and key escutcheons can be cast easily in the workshop by using a car-body repair kit or a resin-casting solution bought from a model shop. Remove one of the original plates and press it face down into a flattened piece of modelling clay to make a clean impression for a mold. Carefully lift the original plate from the modelling clay and then pour in the prepared solution or resin. Do not worry if it overflows or looks too thick; once hardened it is easy to sand. As the resin sets a chemical reaction takes place, causing heat which makes the modelling clay stick to the cast. Usually your impression will have been made before this happens. Once the cast is removed from the mold, brush off the sticky modelling clay with an old toothbrush and white spirit. With a file, remove the uneven bits of the cast using the original handle as a guide and then sand the back to remove the extra thickness. Finally paint the copy with a mixture of bronze dust, gold paint and green spirit stain to get a similar color to the original plate. This method provides a temporary solution for making missing parts to ormolu casts as well. However, the resin is not very strong so in the case of handles the best solution is to cast the back plate and then replace the drop handles and their fixing pins

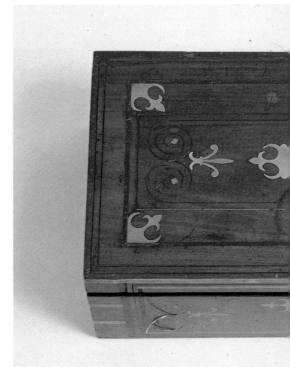

Below: A 19th-century rosewood box inlaid with brass.

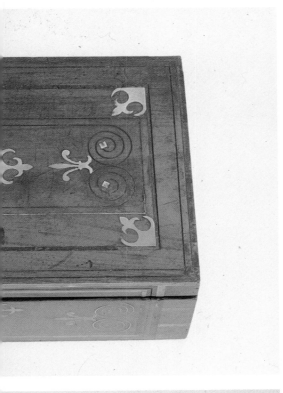

Bottom: Two methods of casting new back or key plates. The first employs gelatine and is accurate and reusable. The second is to simply press the original plate into modelling clay. The casts are shown rough, cleaned, and stained. Far right is the original brass.

with metal reproductions.

Bent metal handles and distorted brass inlay When you find a slight bend in old handles it is tempting to try and force it back to shape by hand. Sometimes this works but as brass becomes very brittle with age it can snap in your hands. Fix the handle in the vise and run a blow torch over the area until it becomes dull. Lift the handle from the vise with a pair of pliers and plunge it into cold water. The metal should now be sufficiently malleable to be bent back to shape.

Fine strips of brass inlay often work loose from their grooves and get bent if not immediately repaired. It is usually possible to reset the brass stringing with hide glue as long as the dirt is cleaned from the groove beforehand. Badly buckled sections have to be removed from their grooves and the damaged area heated and reshaped by the annealing process described above. Removing the brass stringing takes great patience. Flatten and taper the end of a fine metal knitting needle to the width of the groove so that it looks like a tiny shallow-ground chisel. With this instrument work along under the brass stringing and carefully lift the whole section out. It is essential to keep the needle almost flat to the surface of the wood, too steep an angle will cause the metal to curl and sometimes takes parts of the surrounding surface with it. If you come across an obstinate bit of glue, gently heat the tip of the needle (so that it is just too hot to touch) and continue pushing along the groove. Try to avoid the use of solvents to melt the glue, they inevitably spill out from the narrow channel and affect the French polish. When the whole section is free, heat up the damaged area of the brass, plunge it into the water and lightly hammer it flat on a smooth metal surface. Where the sections have twisted as well as buckled, first remove the twists with a pair of pliers before tapping flat. Remember that at this stage the brass is very soft and will get easily marked by the pliers. Heavy blows from the hammer will also cause it to thicken sideways so that it will not fit back into the groove. Do a test run to see if it will bed down properly and then reglue, being sure to clean out any dirt or old adhesive from the groove.

Wider types of brass strip, often found on the edges of rosewood boxes and tables, are usually pinned as well as glued. To lift the section clear you will need two thin metal kitchen knives. Work up to the pin with one knife and then insert the other on the other side, gently lifting the brass strip and pin with it. Once the pin has lifted slightly, push the brass flat again. There should be sufficient pin showing to grip it with the pliers and pull it out.

Replacing missing fancy brass inlay, apart from stringing, is a job for those with plenty of patience. The most common form is the fleur-de-lis. To reproduce such a shape, take an impression of the grave by placing a piece of paper over the recess and gently rubbing the edges with a pencil. Once you have the outline you can now make a kind of sandwich by gluing the paper to a brass sheet of the correct thickness and then backing the other side of the brass with a $\frac{1}{4}$-inch thick square of hardwood. Now for the tricky bit! With your 'sandwich' fixed in the vise, carefully cut slightly outside the pencil line with a fine-bladed fret saw. The wood backing should stop the brass sheet from vibrating. Once your shape is free drop it into some water to soak off the wood and paper. Clean out the grave and by constant testing file the brass to shape so that it fits exactly. If you are extremely accurate you will not need to file. Glue the inlay in place and clamp it flat with the surrounding wood surface. I like to put a thick strip of plastic between the clamp and the surface so that I can see if the brass is bedding down flat. Once the glue has set it is impossible to file the brass flat if it stands proud of the surface without damaging the surrounding wood finish.

Hinges, castors and locks An accumulation of dirt and rust is the most common problem with these metal parts. A light oiling with penetrating oil cures most problems. Except for hinges, which form a part of the decoration on the outside of a piece of furniture, the majority of badly broken types can be replaced from a local supplier. One type which is not readily available is the snipe hinge, found on antique boxes and coffers. These can be reproduced by bending two long and round nails into a 'U' shape – heat them up first as described above. Now you have to make the circle by hammering the nails round a former (the chuck end of an old $\frac{1}{2}$-inch drill bit will do) so that you have a miniature magnifying-glass shape. File the handle ends of these magnifying glasses to a sharp point so that they can then be sunk into the wood. First of all you have to fit the two nails together like a Chinese metal puzzle, one half goes into the coffer lid and the other into the base.

Castors come in a variety of shapes depending on the age of the piece of furniture. The older types either have a bucket arrangement into which the wooden leg fits or simply a long screw projecting from a metal baseplate. Removing and replacing the latter type can be a bit puzzling as initially the wheel just turns in your hand when you try to unscrew the long projection from the table leg. By removing the three small fixing screws and by inserting a long bladed screwdriver into one of these holes it is often possible to jam the blade against the wheel and so provide enough torque to turn the large screw free of the wood. By reversing the direction of pressure such a

Above: Bent and twisted brass stringing.

Below left: Ward locks. The top row shows two of the simplest types. The plate has been levered off the right-hand one to show the action. The bottom row shows two wards fitted with a lever action. The lever has been removed in the right-hand lock.
Below right: Lever locks. Top row; with and without the levers. Bottom; box lock, cheap lever lock.

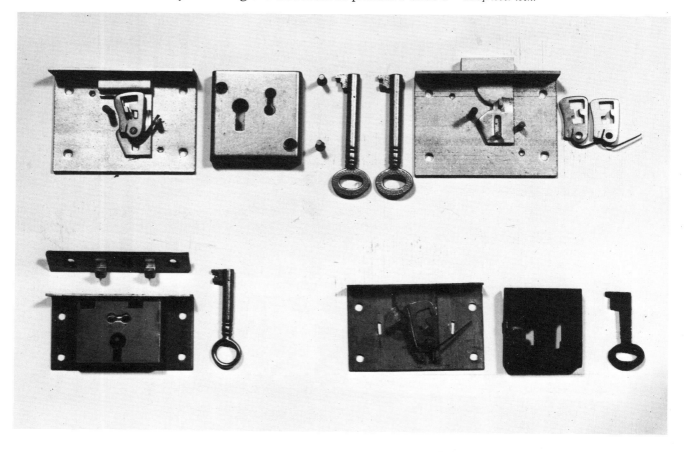

Above: Fitting a folding top hinge.
Below: The old hinge marks have to be packed with end-grain timber before fitting the reproduction hinge.

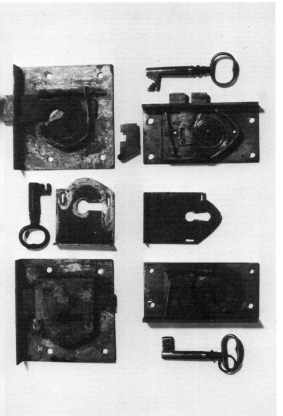

method can be used for fitting the new castor.

The arrangement of locks varies from piece to piece, but there are three main types. The cupboard lock is the type that is fixed to the inside surfaces of doors on furniture. Its action is such that when the key is turned it shoots a bolt sideways into the other door or, in the case of single-doored corner cupboards, into the sideframe. The drawer lock is fitted to the inside edges of drawers and here the bolt rises upward out of the mechanism to lock into the drawer dividers. The box lock comes in two parts – the locking plate which is fixed to the lid of the box, and the lock itself which is recessed, in the manner of the drawer lock, into the front of the box. As the lid of the box is closed the two loops of the locking plate drop into recesses in the lock and these are engaged by teeth when the key is turned.

Locks often get jammed through an accumulation of rust and fluff. Four screws are the standard method of fixing the lock to the wood and these should be carefully removed and replaced afterward. Once the lock is free, turn it over and look at how the casing which covers the mechanism is fixed on. Screws can be easily removed but on early types the backing plate has to be tapped free of its two small rivets. Clean the mechanism out and test it before returning the casing.

Cutting a key and fitting it to work the lock sounds complicated but on antiques, locks are fairly simple. Modern types of locks vary considerably but you can usually buy a complete replacement without the need to repair the existing one. The two main types of antique lock are the ward lock, found on eighteenth-century furniture, and the lever lock. To cut a new key for the first type is relatively simple. The key itself is hollow so that when it is inserted in the lock it centers on a pin. The working part of the key has a series of slots which run in the same direction as the key shank. These slots are designed to fit over a series of protruding metal flanges, called wards, which are fixed to the interior of the lock. Providing the key matches the wards, it turns and engages a halfcircle cut in the bolt. The bolt is shot out and then the key passes back to its original position. Key blanks can be bought; take the lock with you and make sure that the hollow of the key fits the pin exactly. By filing out the slots in the blank to match the wards a new key can be made to work.

Nineteenth-century lever locks are more complicated. The key and bolt arrangement is the same but here levers are fixed on top of the bolt and these have to be pushed aside by the key in order to free the bolt. The teeth on the key run at a right angle to the shank and they should be cut to match the levers. Where you find three levers you will obviously need three teeth or prongs on your key. If you get stuck consult the illustrations, they explain the action far better than words can.

Coloring brass replacements to match One problem with reproduction replacements and brass repairs is that frequently the metal looks too new. Reproduction handles come covered in a solution of murky shellac to give that antique affect. If they do not match, this polish should be stripped off with methylated spirit or paint remover and the brass tarnished by either of the following solutions which can be brushed on over a period of days to achieve the desired effect.

1 part salt	1 part salt
1 part wine vinegar	3 parts copper carbonate
1 part sugar	1 part sal ammoniac
	1 part cream of tartar
	8 parts strong vinegar

REPAIRING SURFACES and FINISHES

Most restoration work you come across will fall into this area. However, if you set about restoring a piece of furniture which is missing part of its carcass or has a broken element, the finishing stage will be the last – first carry out any structural repairs, then move on to damage to veneer, carving or moldings and finally, restore the finish.

Always, where possible, use old and ready patinated wood for replacing missing veneer and edgings on antique furniture, it makes all the difference to producing an invisible repair. Use scrap parts from furniture which is beyond repair and work 'backward' – sand the back off the replacement piece of wood until it gradually drops level with the existing surface. Restoring antique walnut is an example where this approach is essential. The wood fades beautifully, so it is hard to copy this effect with stains.

Dents, bruises and scratches Dents and bruises can be raised by applying a soaked cloth over the area and using localized heat. First strip off the finish around the dent. Put the damp cloth exactly over the dent and on top put a metal cap (from a screw-top bottle) on the cloth over the dent area and heat the cap with a soldering iron until the wood swells back into position. If the bruising is too severe and the cell structure of the wood has been crushed, the only remedy is to fill the hole with shellac stick. You will find that most scores and dents occur in the softer woods like pine and Honduras mahogany.

Deep scratches can be lifted in the same way as bruises. However, patching with a shellac stick is usually the best way of filling scratches before you begin polishing. Hold the shellac stick flat against a heated knife and dribble the shellac into the scratch. When it is set, clean down level to the wood surface. Particularly bad scratches can be patched with a diamond-shaped piece of wood as described in the section on veneer.

Damaged and bruised corners This usually occurs on the top edges of table-top corners. Valuable antique oak furniture should not have these rounded and bruised corners replaced. On mahogany types and modern pieces a piece can be dropped into the corner. Take the cut only halfway down the thickness of the board if possible and

1, 2 and 3. Restoring a bad repair to a bruised table corner. The repair cut was cleaned flush and a new piece of mahogany laid in. It helps to forget about the excess wood and to concentrate on getting the patch perfect. The excess can always be cut flush once the glue has set.

4, 5, 6 and 7. Shaping and marking the cutter to conform with the molding. The remaining portion of the molding is used as a guide and the cutter filed to shape. It is then used in the scratch stock and the new piece of molding spliced on once veneer repairs have been effected.

8. Badly smashed solid moldings can have a new piece spliced in. The replacement block can then be shaped to conform.

9. A new block of wood laid into a broken table top prior to carving.

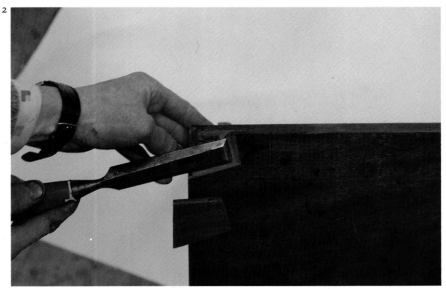

4

5

glue the new section in. Where the whole corner is missing, a piece has to be spliced on diagonally across the table-top grain.

Cigarette and scorch marks in wood Rarely does this form of damage affect only the polish; in most cases the burn goes right down into the wood. By gluing a patch of sandpaper on the end of a $\frac{1}{4}$-inch dowel rod the black and charred section can be partially removed without affecting the rest of the polish. A drop of oxalic acid will often lighten the burn even further. Once dry, the hole can be patched and levelled with some shellac stick.

Molding repairs and replacements Small sections of molding can be produced with the scratch stock as described in the tool section. File your scratch stock to shape and take a board of the appropriate wood, and scratch out your molding with the edge. Once the profile and length is correct, cut the molding from the board. Large moldings of over 2 inches can be done in two sections with the scratch stock and then joined together. Solid moldings which form the edges of table tops should have their heavily damaged section cut out as illustrated. A new block is dropped in, and once the glue has dried it can then be carved or scratched to shape.

6

8

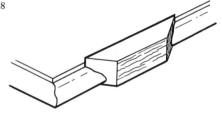

7

9

Carving repairs On better quality furniture carving can take some pretty elaborate forms. Envisage the carving in its simplest form and then cut out the basic shape with a coping saw. It is then a lot easier to work once the basic outline is glued to the furniture. With all carving, you have to be aware of grain direction. If your cut starts to splinter, work from the opposite direction. Small carved edges to table tops often need to have parts of their sections replaced. If used carefully a razor-sharp scalpel will cut through the most brittle timbers to give you the outline. Such tools need careful handling and must not be forced. Finishing the surface can be done with fine sandpaper wrapped around an appropriate block, shaped to conform to the carving.

Below: A Victorian oak sideboard carved with scenes from Robinson Crusoe. *It was designed and carved by Gerald Robinson in Newcastle, England.*

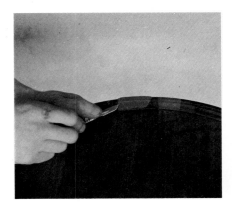

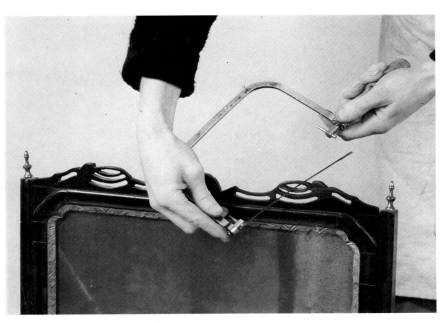

Above: Using the flexible nature of a scalpel blade to add the finishing states to a replacement molding. These blades are not designed for wood and at all times gentle pressure should be used and protective eye goggles worn.

Right: The top fretwork on this ebonized mirror has had one section replaced. Light colored shapes always look larger than dark ones so it can help to put one coat of stain on prior to finishing by eye. In this case the fretwork shapes were still too big. A coping saw was fed through and its fairly rigid blade used as a sander.

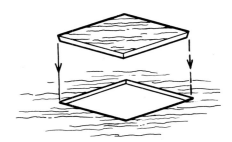

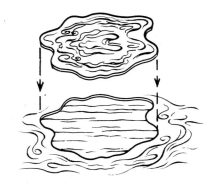

Above: Methods of patching missing veneer. Inconspicuous repairs rely on patching with the grain. On straight-grained timber, the diamond patch is used: Burl woods require an irregular shape. This looks complicated, but the grave can easily be pared back with a scalpel.

Veneer The idea of applying a beautifully marked layer of wood onto a cheap and less attractive timber base goes back 3000 years, to ancient Egypt. As an alternative technique to solid-wood construction it first appeared in England in the 1660s and since then it has been used on many forms of furniture.

Veneer problems Veneer which has lifted is perhaps the easiest problem to sort out because no replacements are required. First, clean out the underside with a scalpel, insert some new glue under the veneer and clamp with a piece of waxed paper and a block of wood. A blister in the center of a piece of veneer has to be split with a scalpel. Use a fine artist's brush or a syringe to get new glue in under the veneer. Alternatively, you can strip off the surrounding polish and apply a damp cloth and an iron set at a moderate heat (nylon or wool setting) – the old cabinet glue will reamalgamate with heat and moisture and the pressure from the iron will smooth out the blister. The first method, using the scalpel, leaves the most invisible repair because the polished surface is left untouched and is preferable in most cases. If the old glue has set in a solid crust under the blister and proves difficult to clean out, before applying the new glue you can cut out the blister with the scalpel, then clean out the glue and reglue the piece of veneer in its grave. To achieve an invisible repair when bits of veneer are missing you must be aware of which way the grain runs in the piece. The illustrations show how the diamond patch is used for straight grain but an irregular shape is better for burl woods like walnut. To get a perfect fit, first make a template of the damaged area by taking a rubbing with pencil and paper, cut this shape out and then lay it on the new piece of veneer. By aligning the grain direction on the new veneer with that of the original grain a diamond patch can be drawn out, just covering the damaged area. Cut your patch out of the veneer with angled cuts as illustrated and then place the shape over the missing part. By using this as a guide for the blade you can then cut the lines for making the grave in the original surface. In this way you get a perfect fit every time.

Some people like to cut the grave first and then cut the veneer to fit but this method requires experience and an eye for accuracy. On antique pieces where the veneer is thicker than the modern type and you do not have any old veneer you should use two layers to build it up to the original level. Occasionally, you come across veneer that runs vertically (as on drawer dividers on a chest of drawers) and you should use a square instead of the scant splice. If the whole top of a veneered piece is damaged by a large number of blisters a wet cloth and hot iron will lift the whole sheet free. In such cases the surface is probably ruined anyway so the damp cloth will do little extra damage.

By using the technique described in counterveneering warped tables, the old veneer can be relaid or a new piece applied. Both surfaces must be clean and dry. Slightly score the top of the table and the underside of the veneer with the edge of a saw and apply hot cabinet glue to both the ground and the veneer. When the glue becomes tacky the veneer can be applied to the ground and the top surface dampened with a cloth. Run an iron over the surface to remelt the glue. Before the glue sets again, press a piece of smooth hardwood over the center and work out toward the edges in a zigzag fashion forcing the excess glue and air bubbles out. The traditional tool is called a veneer hammer. Keep on resoaking and reheating the veneer if the glue starts to set while you are working on the surface with the hardwood block but do not flood the veneer with too much water – if you are returning the original veneer it should fit exactly up to the edges. If it goes over the edges it means you have applied too much water and when it dries out the boards beneath the veneer will warp.

Modern veneering methods use very thin veneer which is applied with a contact adhesive and a roller (instructions on veneering come with the adhesive), but up until the 1930s most veneers were applied and fixed with the old cabinet glue.

Replacing antique veneer on curved and shaped surfaces
It is easy to clamp loose or replacement veneer down on flat surfaces, even in the center of a table top where a patch holder can be used (*see page 41*) but problems arise in holding veneer in place on molded sur-

Below: Using a shaped pine block to hold veneer to curved surfaces. Where thick veneer has been used it can help to steam-bend the replacement veneer around a similar curve (an old paint tin, for example). When dry, the wood will be curved, and can be fixed with ease.

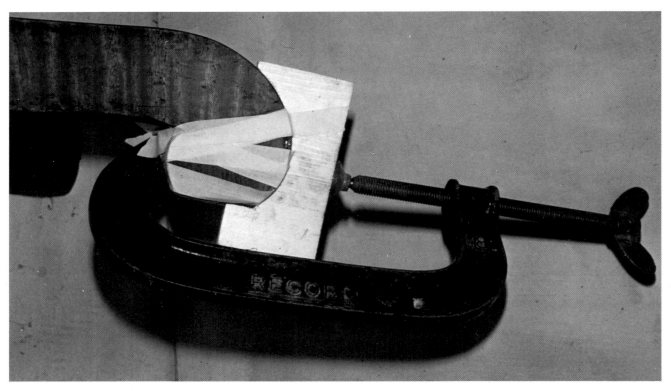

faces and rounded edges. On concave-shaped surfaces such as moldings on the bottom of a veneered chest of drawers, one old method was to carve an exact mirror image of the molding in pine. This was then clamped and used as a press to hold the veneer down while the glue set. A faster method is to take an impression of the molding (further along from the damaged area where the molding is intact) in modelling clay. Carefully free the modelling clay and construct a cardboard frame around it, into which you should pour plaster of Paris. When the plaster is set you have an exact replica of the molding. Now tape up the plaster square with card as you did with the modelling clay and apply a shellac coat to the first plaster cast and then pour in more plaster of Paris; when dry free it from its mate. You now have a mirror image of the molding which can be used as a press while the repaired veneer is setting.

Convex shapes, where the veneer has to be bent outward, can have the facings of wood secured by cutting out a softening block as illustrated and clamping it to the veneer to hold it in place. Thin modern veneer can be fixed to curved surfaces by using one of the contact cements, but you have to thoroughly soak the veneer and leave it clamped around a curved surface until it dries into shape. Subsequent contact gluing is made a lot easier if the veneer already has curve to it.

Below and right : Plaster of Paris is excellent for acting as a veneer press to hold veneer to curved surfaces until the glue dries. A plasticine wall can be built on a sound section and the plaster poured in. A light smear of grease should be applied beforehand and the plaster removed before it has fully dried. Plaster produces heat as it sets, so it can leave a bloom mark. This method, while faster than the double cast described in the text, should not be used on antiques.

Stringing and inlay repairs Inlays of exotic and colorful woods set into solid-wood backgrounds have been used since the sixteenth century in Europe for decorative furniture. The technique for replacing missing patches is exactly the same as that described in the chapter on metal repairs. By laying a piece of paper over the empty grave an impression can be formed and a new piece cut and dropped in. Long lines of black and white box or sycamore stringing inlaid into solid and veneered surfaces is a feature particularly associated with the late eighteenth and early nineteenth century.

Standard lengths and widths of stringing can be bought from wood suppliers, but making your own is simply a matter of constructing a stringing planer as described in the tool section. Cut off a flat section from your lump of box wood with a stiff-bladed tenon saw, square strips can then be cut and fed through the planer until they conform to size. When you replace the damaged section with your new length try to avoid the use of butt joints. The long splice makes a far better mend.

Complicated arrangements of squares and stringing lines to be found in the edges of antique tables look as if they would take hours to repair. Although it appears as if they were all laid individually the technique used for both making and repairing them is to glue lengths of stringing and veneer around a center block so that when this fattened block is viewed from its 'end grain' an exact pattern of the missing section is produced. A slice is then taken off the end of the block to produce the border. A fine saw should be used to cut off these sections so as not to splinter the glued parts. If the initial glue job is done well the slice will hold together no matter how thin your sliced off section is.

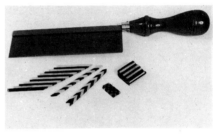

Top: Using tape to hold stringing in place.
Above center: Using the folding wedge method to clamp box and ebony strips together to form the basis of decorative inlay. The wedge is driven in the direction of the arrow.
Above: Lengths can then be cut at the appropriate angle. By reversing one strip, a chevron effect is achieved. The first cut is the type of inlay used on the chest to the right.

Left: Early-19th century 'Tunbridge ware' tray. These articles are made by gluing lengths of shaped wood or stringing together as illustrated in the chequered block above. This is then cut at a right angle to produce a veneer, which is mounted on a solid-wood base.

Right: A Scandinavian Empire chest decorated with marquetry. The top section is a 20th-century addition to make the piece look like a secretaire *from the Austrian Biedermeier period. (Desks always sell better than chests.) Rosewood has been used instead of the matching curls of mahogany on the base. Note that the leaves are much more angular on the marquetry top. The piece should in fact look like a marquetry version of the chest illustrated on page 25.*

Marquetry repairs Marquetry differs in technique from inlay. Although they initially look similar, marquetry consists of hundreds of pieces of veneer laid onto a pine or oak ground to cover the complete surface. In fact it is a complicated form of veneer and, unlike inlay, none of the background appears. Most marquetry pieces are antique and despite the fact that some of them have borax carcasses they are always valuable. Missing sections can be replaced by taking an impression. Follow the techniques described in metal repairs and inlay. The back edges of the new patch should be slightly tapered

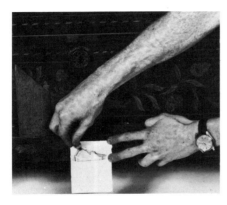

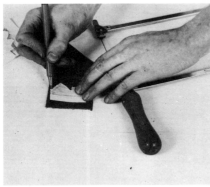

Top: In marquetry repairs the shape of missing pieces is ascertained by using paper and a soft pencil. The edges bruise very easily.
Center: When working close to furniture in a detailed job like this, it is easy to forget about grain direction. Lay the new piece of wood alongside and then mark it.
Above: The marked shape can then be cut with a fret saw. If the veneer is very thin, clamp it in a sandwich of two thicker pieces.
Right: The piece in place. The excess can be cut off later with a mini-hacksaw blade held in the hand. The black and white border to the drawers (not the stringing) is not original. The design is too crude to match the delicate floral marquetry.

as this makes a tighter fit. Occasionally you might find the type that has slight gaps between each section. To make your repairs in keeping, such a gap should be left between the new sections and the old and then filled with oak grain filler or a mixture of fine sawdust, brown-umber powder color, and glue. The excess can be wiped and levelled with the surface before it sets.

On some types of marquetry a two-dimensional effect is achieved on pieces of veneer which form a fan arrangement, either at the center or corners of table tops and fall-fronts to bureaus. Each segment of the fan shape has one edge, tip and outer portion a slightly darker color than the center. This effect is not produced by stain, but by the technique known as sand shading. Before final shaping and laying, the edge of each segment is dipped into fine sand, heated up on a tin placed on a low heat. When it comes to replacing these types you can easily get this effect yourself by using the same method. Always do a test run on a piece of spare veneer of the same species to see how long you need to leave the piece in the sand. It is very easy to get a burned rather than a shaded effect. Be prepared for a long and involved job when it comes to restoring marquetry and if you have a valuable piece consult an expert before starting repairs.

Unless you happen to be using already patinated wood and are working the back off each replacement part until it is level with the surrounding surfaces, you will find it difficult with all the above surface repairs to get your patches of new wood level with the surface without marking the polish of surrounding wood. Diamond patching which has been used in solid surfaces to fill a bad bruise can be levelled initially with a small bull-nose plane and then finished off level. In all cases the cabinet scraper is ideal, as it can be bent in the fingers and used to level the patch without affecting the surrounding polish. You might find you have to work in two directions to get an even and level effect. This tool becomes easier to use with experience. If you cannot master it, a Stanley-knife blade with its edge slightly turned over can be held between the forefinger and thumb and pushed along to reduce the thickness of the patch. Unfortunately these blades are not flexible, so as you approach the finished level to get the patch in line with the surface, the edge of the blade cuts into the original wood. Continual practice with the cabinet scraper on scrap wood is the best solution before trying it on furniture.

Above and top: Staining a replacement to a 17th-century oak table top. The various stains are patched on using the wood as a palette and not mixed beforehand. The medullary rays can be simulated by sharpening a wax candle to pencil shape and drawing in the lines. The stain will not affect these areas. Good carpentry work is often ruined by overstaining or by smearing the stain onto original surfaces in order to blend the new piece in. This is not necessary and parts look far better understained.

Staining and matching replacements Along with the materials mentioned in the chapter on tools you will need various sizes of good-quality paint brushes for making your repairs invisible. Small brushes of either sable or squirrel are ideal for touching up grain patterns.

Coloring replacement parts is a lot easier if you mix your pigments and stains yourself. Surface colors of wood are rarely uniform, the overall color of say, old oak, is often composed of yellows, greens and browns. Do not buy a readymade oak stain and expect to get an exact match. Closely examine the existing wood around your patch and try to break the uniform color down into basic components. By seeing 'below the surface,' so to speak, and working out the base color, an exact match can often be made by dabbing various totally different stains on to the new wood with absorbent cotton. Start with the light colors such as yellow and work up the scale, constantly referring to the original surface. Initially this effect looks pretty strange and rather drastic but when you put on the last color it combines with the others to make a perfect match. Instead of combining your colors beforehand, you are actually using the wood as the palette.

Stains and dyes As a general guide, patchings and solid-wood carpentry repairs show up lighter than the existing surfaces. They consequently have to be stained down. Vandyke brown crystals or powder have to be recommended as a universal stain for antique furniture replacements. Depending on the strength of the mix, an extraordinary range of colors, from pale-walnut brown to almost pure black, can be made from this one stain alone. Both the crystals and the powder are mixed up with warm water to produce the stain. The powder first has to be combined with ammonia to form a paste before adding water. Grain swelling can be avoided on some types of wood if the replacement surfaces are first wetted and then lightly sanded with the finest glass paper before applying the water stain.

Spirit-soluble aniline dyes are also excellent for staining small replacements. These are dissolved in methylated spirits in the workshop and fixed by adding a teaspoonful of French polish to every pint made. They produce a particularly subtle effect but tend to fade over long periods when used on large areas. Oil stains are excellent for modern pieces though they do not play a large part in antique repairs. Some leather-shoe stains containing naptha provide a permanent and strong color for woods like mahogany and oak. Red and black are the two most readily available colors and by mixing the two a nice warm-brown tone can be made. Combined with spirit stains, they often stop the former from fading.

You can often get a natural shine to the wood by closing the grain before polishing with a smooth metal object such as the back of a spoon or gouge chisel. This technique, known as burnishing or boning in, works particularly well on small areas of half-round molding and small veneer patches. Do not burnish large surfaces as it can bruise the wood. Cabinetmakers in the 1920s often used the dried rib of an ox for burnishing larger surfaces and closing up the grain.

With antiques try rubbing a cake of pure beeswax over the newly stained sections and then take the most part of it off before French polishing with fine steel wool. This leaves a deposit in the grain which acts as the filler. Where spirit stains have been used this light coat of wax prevents the French polish from ripping out the color.

Lightening and bleaching replacements If you are restoring pale-colored woods, and your replacements are too dark, they can be lightened with either oxalic-acid crystals dissolved in water or with one of the recent two-part bleaching packs. One solution of the two-part type contains an alkali which pulls the natural color of the wood to the surface, this is then lifted out by the second solution, a powerful form of bleach. Oxalic acid is not quite as severe as these packs and consequently it can be controlled to a greater extent.

The problem with all bleaching is that it leaves the wood lifeless and without depth. Subsequent staining to match results in a dull, matt effect. One solution is to stop the action of the bleach when it fades the wood to the right color. Staining becomes unnecessary and a covering of polish is all that is required. Be careful of a table top that has been left outside if the surface has gone pale due to continual soaking and drying out. The wood will be incredibly absorbent and if you stain as soon as the wood is dry, the fibers suck the stain right in to produce a nasty matt effect. The tripod table in chapter six had its color restored by four hours of hand waxing. In most cases the color lies just below the surface. Initially the water darkens the wood and unless an object is left standing on the top it evaporates and dries off in an even fashion. Simple waxing pulls the color back out again. Natural fading on antique furniture is highly prized. Over the years walnut goes a beautiful honey color or pale gray, Honduras mahogany a pale orange and rosewood a golden yellow.

Pigment colors These tend to obscure the grain rather than enhance it. Basically they are simply powder colors miscible in either water or oil and are useful as a base for paint patching and for obscuring bad burn marks.

Chemical staining The darkening effect of chemical agents is produced by the chemical combining with the acids in the woods. Most of these chemicals are alkaline in nature. The most common type used in the restoration of mahogany is bichromate of potash. This comes in the form of orange crystals which are steeped in warm water and then painted on the wood. If the solution is strong, the drying process leaves a coating of bright yellow which can be burnished off to reveal the darkening effect. Ammonia will darken oak. Both these types should only be used for darkening replacement pieces and not as an overall stain for antique pieces.

Fixing stains and French polishing The more dense a material is, the greater the likelihood of achieving a deep shine. Heavy woods like ebony which consist of 80 percent wood fiber and 20 percent air will take on an amazing gloss appearance with one coat of polish. At the other end of the scale, woods like balsa which are 80 percent air require several coats before any kind of depth can be achieved. In all polishing the secret lies in filling the grain of the wood until a hard and completely flat casing is laid around the surface. Replacements to antique parts should be French polished to build up their surface and fill the woodgrain.

French polish is simply shellac with various hardeners and gums added to a base of alcohol or industrial spirits. Historically, the earliest finishes for wood were either a simple waxing or an oil varnishing made by dissolving copal resin in Linseed oil or poppy oil. By the middle of the seventeenth century shellac made by dissolving lac in spirits of wine became popular. The technique of French polishing appeared in the 1820s and gradually replaced other finishes.

French polishing takes a little time to learn and it is recommended that you first practice on scrap timber. First of all you have to make a polisher's pad, or rubber, by taking a piece of absorbent cotton and folding it into a firm egg-shaped pad. A pointed end and a blunted, round end should be made. This pad is then wrapped in a small square

Above: Faded rosewood is one of the most difficult woods to restore. Nearly all the members of the family are dark when first cut but fade beautifully with time. In some cases it can help to use a pale Honduras mahogany as the base and to simulate the grain by chemical means. A fairly convincing effect can be achieved by dissolving Potassium Dichromate crystals in water and using as a stain. Initially, as the water evaporates, the crystals re-form, resulting in an obscuring yellow effect. These can be lifted with steel wool and the strength of color tested by burnishing. By starting with a weak solution and gradually working up the scale the whole range of colored stripes can be simulated.

of old but clean linen, such as a handkerchief. Gather up the cloth around the absorbent cotton and twist it slightly by hand; the rubber should be held so that the thick end rests under the palm while the pointed end is guided by the forefinger. Before starting polishing, your table top should be thoroughly clean, the workshop warm and dust free. Open the pad and pour the French polish in from the back, not through the cloth at the front. Rewrap the rubber and press it against a smooth surface to bring the polish to the front. Avoid over-filling the rubber with polish, too much can cause it to pile up on the surface. Start to cover the surface in a series of straight lines and then work in circles and figures of eight. It is important to bring the pad into contact and off the surface as if you were landing a model air-plane held in the hand. Plunking the rubber down or lifting it straight off results in a marred surface. Do not expect immediate results, it is a slow process. If the surface appears a bit rough after the first coat it can be rubbed down with fine pumice powder applied to a rag, or run over with fine steel wool.

All the fine dust from this operation has to be wiped off before carrying on to the next coat. Your pad has to be replenished from time to time. Polish until the grain in the wood is completely filled. By continually sanding with pumice between coats, the grain fills up without having a thick coating of polish. Allow at least half an hour between coats; it is a good idea to make a new rubber while waiting. When working the polish, a dab of oil can be placed on the rubber (white polishing oil or linseed will do). Do not use too much as in the later stages the oil can prove difficult to remove. Smears left by the oil can be pulled out by pouring some methylated spirits into the rubber and continuing work by rubbing a little harder than before in a figure of eight. All work should be left for 24 hours before the final waxing.

Renovating the existing finish Very often it is possible to clean furniture surfaces up and renovate the finish without having to strip the piece completely. While water is not good for wood, a slightly moistened cloth charged with a small amount of household scouring powder works wonders for removing dirt and rarely stays long

French polishing:
1. Laying out the rubber.
2. Making the pad into a mouse shape.
3. The French polish is poured in from the back of the rubber.
4. The polish is brought to the surface by pressing the rubber against the hand.
5. The rubber is worked first in straight lines and then a figure eight movement.

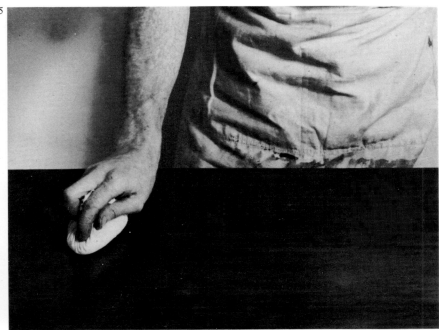

enough to affect the work. Once the piece is clean you might see that the polish has become crazed or rather dry looking in places. Often this can be rectified by applying one of the revivers previously mentioned (*see page 49*). Such homemade solutions have to be well shaken before being applied and wiped off with a cloth. Continuous rubbing over affected areas will return their gloss.

Patches of missing French polish can be filled by going over the area with the rubber. Use a cork block covered in fine wet-and-dry paper to remove the finish that builds up on the existing one. As you carry on through the processes the new French polish builds up to the level of the old.

White water marks in polish The disadvantage of shellac and French polish finishes is that they become easily marked by heat and moisture. White water marks are not too serious and can usually be removed with elbow grease and some automobile metal polish. Work this sparingly into the area with a cloth until the white mark disappears. The effect is instantaneous and the mark disappears completely, but it can return after about 10 minutes. In this case it is best to add a little linseed oil to the polish.

Below: White water marks on a Chinese hardwood stand, circa 1860.
Bottom: The mark is removed with metal polish and linseed oil.
Below left: The finished piece.

Black stains These are caused by water or spirits penetrating right through the polish and down into the wood. They are a lot harder to remove as the polish has to be stripped from the area and oxalic acid applied to the mark. Frequently you just have to accept them – apart from drastic sanding there is no real solution. AB bleaching kits will sometimes lift most of the mark.

Restoring the 'antique' finish This finish has nothing whatsoever to do with the natural patination and depth of color to be found on the real antique. It is an invention of the Victorian era mainly used on oak furniture to make it look old. It became a very popular finish in the latter half of the nineteenth century and through the Edwardian period for mass-produced, machine-carved pieces. A stain was suspended in French polish or varnish and the coats were laid on and highlights rubbed off to produce a scuffed antique look. As the varnish itself is actually colored, such finishes completely hide the grain of the wood and where bits have chipped off the wood shows up as yellowy-white. Patches can be restored by mixing a brown umber pigment powder to a naptha oil stain with a little gold size added as a binder. This can then be painted on and French polished. Antiquing kits can be bought readymade for this purpose though the majority of them are used as an overall finish.

Restoring fumed oak furniture This finish was popular in England in the 1920s and 1930s. Unfinished oak was exposed to ammonia fumes until it went a yellow golden color. First glue your replacement parts to the furniture by using hide glue and a layer of thin paper between the join. This allows you to carve or shape the piece exactly to fit and then remove it by inserting a thin-bladed knife down the gap made by the paper. Pour the strongest type of ammonia into a saucer and place the saucer in an airtight plastic bag with your piece of wood. The fumes will start to color the oak almost immediately. Keep checking for color but take a deep breath before looking in the bag and always wear gloves to remove the wood. Ammonia fumes are particularly irritating to the lungs and skin. Once the right shade is reached permanently glue the piece back on and finish with wax.

Never use ammonia on antique furniture as an overall finish. It can turn the wood a nasty deep-red or chocolate-brown color. It is used in restoration for removing antique casein paint in bad areas prior to rebuilding the surface and for fuming drawer carcass replacements. If you have to make a new drawer for an antique piece the oak base, back and sides can be placed in the plastic back prior to gluing the piece up. The fumes darken the wood and give a better effect than staining.

Restoring antique painted furniture and simulated graining This is one area of restoration where you have to have a natural ability in handling a brush and a good sense of how colors work and combine together. Painting is the oldest and cheapest means of decorating furniture. It has always been a popular finish in America. The majority of antique types, with the exception of some types of Windsor chairs, have a white undercoat applied before painting. This is simply a type of gesso made from whiting (crushed and refined chalk) and size. Mix up some of this mixture to repatch the spaces where the gesso has flaked off and build it up layer by layer until it is just below the level of the original surface. Grind powder colors with a small amount of casein paint glue and add water to thin the mixture. The solution can then be painted on the gesso. Finally, smooth the surface with fine steel wool and wax up. With the recent

Below: An antique painted Regency chair. Bottom: Applying a coat of gesso to a replacement stretcher.

Top: Using a variety of stains to coat the gesso.

Above: It is essential not to use sandpaper on the gesso groundwork when repairing chairs such as this Windsor chair. If you look closely, the brush marks in the original paint often still show the stain or color. This stretcher is approaching the finishing stages.

craze for stripping furniture down to the wood few antique painted pieces have survived. They are valuable if the paint is original so always take such pieces to the professional until you get familiar with basic color theory.

Windsor chairs have their paints laid directly onto the wood. On the seat, back, spindles and arms this gets worn away and is a particularly pleasing feature. I prefer to simply wax such pieces and leave them as they are. Simulated graining is either applied directly onto the wood and sealed with shellac or applied to a gesso base. Stain the ground work first and then a naptha oil stain (bound with gold size to prevent it running) can be painted on with a fine pencil brush. A light covering of shellac can then be applied. With the gesso-based types, the casein paint mixture can be used. Again in cases where the wear is natural, it is usually a better policy to leave the piece as is.

Lacquer Lacquer is one of the most confusing terms used to describe finishes and decoration for furniture. Basically it covers 4 completely different finishes.

One/Lacquer finish. This is perhaps the most commonly used term and refers to a clear cellulose varnish developed in the early part of this century for factory-line furniture. The base of this finish is highly volatile, its main solvent being acetone or amylacetate. You can distinguish it in its liquid state by its pungent smell. Once sprayed on to furniture it dries in seconds, hence its popularity for mass-produced goods. The only thing that will shift this kind of finish is acetone or lacquer thinner.

Two/Oriental lacquer. This is a built-up pictorial finish developed by the Chinese and perfected by the Japanese centuries ago. It is made from the syrupy sap of a *Rhus venificera* tree. The process is incredibly complicated, requiring the right conditions of heat and humidity. The sap is refined and laid on in layers and sets with the hardness and flexibility of plastic. Once cured, it can withstand temperatures of up to 160 degrees Centigrade and is resistant to acids, alkalis, alcohol and many types of caustics. When imported into Europe it was so expensive that it began to be imitated with a totally different material by the end of the seventeenth century. Damage to most of the modern varieties you come across can be lightly patched in with oil colors.

Three/European and American Lacquer. A more correct term for the type of furniture and techniques used in imitation of Japanese lacquer is Japanning. Since it was impossible for the Europeans to use the same process as Oriental lacquer they turned to shellac as a substitute. This is made from the incrustations on the twigs of trees in India by an insect called *Coccus lacca*. When these deposits are purified they produce the toffee-like substance known as shellac. When steeped in methylated spirits and with the addition of hardening gums it becomes French polish. Japanned furniture is one of the hardest types to restore. To get the raised effect European cabinet-makers used gesso covered with layer upon layer of colored shellac varnish and gold and bronze dust. In the wrong conditions the whole structure of the gesso base deteriorates and attempts at restoration can sometimes lead to the whole surface crumbling beneath your hands. If the base appears sound you can patch in missing areas of raised decoration with gesso. Ordinary oil colors can be used to paint the raised parts. Where bronze or gold dust have been employed the painted area should be lightly covered with gold size and the powder sprinkled on once the surface has become tacky. A thin layer of French polish can then be applied to protect the colors.

Four/Lacquer on tin ware. This was a type of black ware made by coating metal surfaces with black asphaltum varnish which was then baked on in temperatures of up to 300 degrees Centigrade. It does not concern us here since it was mainly used for metalware. However you might find the odd papier-mâché object coated in this material. Build up the damaged areas with a modern paste filler supported on several strips of wire or small cocktail sticks glued into the smashed section. This makes it easier to build up the base before applying a coat of black shellac polish to blend in with the surface. Papier-mâché trays often have their corners smashed off and can be restored in this fashion.

Below: A late 19th-century reproduction chest on gilt wood stand. Although this piece is a reproduction or a 'copy' the Japanning techniques used are traditional. Restoring Japanned furniture is an area into which the beginner should tip toe with extreme caution. A surface will disintegrate completely in inexperienced hands.
The bottom pictures show how small areas can be built up with gesso, gilded and then painted with oil color.

Stripping off existing polishes Sometimes the existing polish and surface of furniture is so badly damaged that you have to strip. The question is what kind of solvent or stripper to use. Most varnishes or polishes have their resins, gums or bases suspended in a solution. When they are painted on, the solution or solvent evaporates leaving a thin dried layer of resin or gum. To get this off you have to find what the original solution or solvent was in order to return the dried polish to a liquid state so that it can be easily removed. Shellac and French polish, the two most common types you are likely to have to strip, can be removed with methylated spirits and fine steel wool. The cellulose and lacquer finish can be removed with amylacetate or lacquer thinner. The old surface just blisters up and can almost be peeled off. The tougher, more modern varnishes such as the urethane types can be lifted off with proprietary paint stripper, though you have to be careful what type you use if you find a modern finish on an antique. The best and most easily controlled types have a thin

Left and Top: The overstripped look can be avoided by cleaning one component at a time. Apply methylated spirits and, once the polish is soft, burnish it off with a dry piece of steel wool. Revivers have to be recommended as an alternative to paint stripper for visible wood surfaces as its action can be stopped before the patina is damaged. The beechwood rocker is the sort of piece the restorer leaves as is.

Above: A 19th-century Boston rocker in the stripping stages. The dirty French polish was softened with methylated spirits and lifted with a flexible palette knife to avoid destroying the original paint underneath.

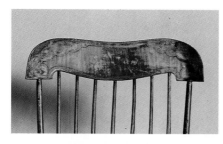

Top and above: The original stencil work to the Boston rocker and oak showing beneath an asphaltum stain.

Below: Casting from a repetition molding to a mirror frame. An undamaged piece of gilding is greased, a modelling-clay wall built, and gelatine poured in (the type used for puddings, made strong in a double boiler). It is essential to allow the gelatine to cool almost to the point of setting before use. Air bubbles are brought to the surface by tapping the frame.
Below center: Once set, the wall can be removed and the gelatine peeled off. A cast is then taken by a mixture of whiting and hot cabinet glue.
Below right: The cast is glued with cabinet glue and its details sharpened.

consistency and this allows you to remove the varnish quickly as it bubbles up and before it has time to soak into the wood. Noncaustic types are the best as they tend not to darken the wood. By concentrating on a small area at a time and judging the right moment to lift off the buckling polish you can completely strip a piece without the wood surface coming into contact with the stripper. In this fashion the grain rarely opens up and does not require filling before repolishing. It is tempting to try to save time on antique pieces by filling the grain with a proprietory grain filler or tinted plaster of Paris. A far better finish can be obtained by patiently using the French polishing process instead, and sanding each coat with finest grade steel wool. In all modern work, when revarnishing with either the tough urethane types or the penetrating wood-sealer variety, manufacturer's instructions should be followed to the letter. Only some kinds of stains can be used with such finishes so it is important to check what type to use before brushing on the varnish.

Gilding There are a variety of techniques to lay gold leaf onto furniture and picture frames. Much of the indoor gilding in the past was carried out by the water-gilding method, but it is a lot easier for the beginner to use the oil method. On small areas it makes no difference to the finished effect. Victorian gilding has a base of yellow color applied to the compo (a hardened and newer version of gesso) before the gold leaf is laid down. Earlier examples employ a red base. You can usually see what type has been used. First of all you have to rebuild the ground work. Compo can be made by mixing liquid resin with plaster of Paris. It is usually built up around a wire core or pinned to the picture frame or furniture. Where a whole section is missing it is often possible to take a cast with modelling clay from a similar shape elsewhere on the piece. This can then be cast and glued to the wire frame, and trimmed up afterward. Gesso, a more delicate technique, has to be laid down in layers and carved once dry. In both cases it is essential to get the groundwork as smooth as possible otherwise specks of dirt and rough patches show up through the gold leaf. Once the part is smoothed to shape, the base color has to be applied by using artist's oil paints – either the red or the yellow

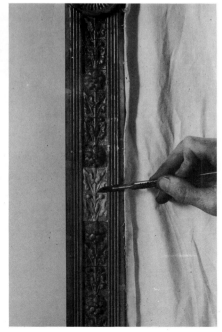

A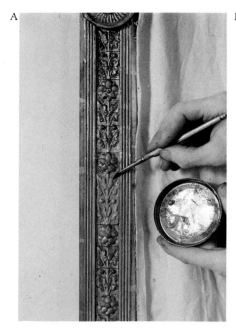

B

C

1

A. The cast is painted with oil paint thinned with liquid drier. B. A coat of gold size is applied and the leaf laid. C. The protective finish is made with water size.

2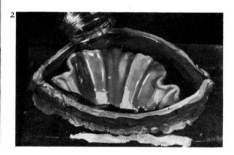

3

4

depending on the age of the piece. Once this is dry it can be smoothed down and the surface inspected for specks of dust. You have to be very particular and it is best at this stage to take the piece out of the workshop into a dust-free atmosphere. Now apply a thin coating of gold size to the part and leave it until it is almost dry. You can test for dryness by coating a spare piece of gesso or compo with gold size and testing this piece with the finger tips. Once dry, take a sheet of gold leaf out of the book (the easiest types to apply come fixed to a thin backing paper) and apply it over the area in one single operation. The thin layer of leaf immediately adheres to the size and pulls away from its paper backing. Now burnish the gold with a really smooth object – the traditional material was a piece of agate. The smoother your original base, the more brilliant will be the result. The ground-work on eighteenth-century gilding on small mirrors and picture frames was so carefully prepared that pieces like these often get passed by at auctions because people think they are new due to their flawless finish. Later and cheaper examples have a rougher ground-work and as it is these types you are likely to come across it makes your job of restoration a lot easier! This whole operation takes quite some time so be prepared for a long though extremely enjoyable job. Do not be put off by the technical terms like compo and gesso. The former can be made as described and the latter is simply whiting and size mixed together. Gold size (a type of turpentine soluble-oil varnish) and paper-backed gold leaf can be obtained from art shops. If they do not stock it they can tell you where to get it. Modern picture frames are painted with gold paint; such paints should never be used on antique gilding.

Ebonizing This technique goes back to the sixteenth century where cheaper varieties of wood were stained and polished to look like ebony. It was particularly popular for furniture during the Edwardian period. Most inexpensive black pianos are ebonized. When making replacements, choose a close-grained wood like pear, apple or maple. French polish is combined with black aniline dyes. Before the 1960s and the advent of petroleum-based plastics all gramophone records were made from shellac. Take one of these broken old records and smash it into small pieces and then steep the pieces overnight in methylated spirits. You get an amazing thick, black varnish that can be applied with a brush and steel wool between coats. It is ideal for black Victorian drawer pulls on chest of drawers.

1. Where there is no pattern to cast from, missing sections can be shaped by eye in plastic clay.
2. This can then be freed and a mold made with gelatine.
3. The plastic clay is freed from the mold and the whiting and glue mixture poured in layer by layer.
4. The new section is returned. Gelatine is so accurate that it even makes a perfect cast of the join line. The replacement is too Art Nouveau and slightly unbalanced. Hand carving and coats of gesso (whiting and size) will give a more baroque feel to the piece before gilding.

Above: Ebonizing a replacement fret work to a mirror top.

Tortoise shell repairs Some small boxes can be found covered in tortoise shell veneer. Where bits of the veneer are missing you have to use tortoise shell for replacements. Fake tortoise shell made from plaster of Paris is a bad compromise. Keep an eye open for badly damaged tortoise shell pieces at auction. Where the veneer has lifted it becomes incredibly stiff and to make it more malleable it is best to remove the whole top and plunge it into hot water. It then becomes very malleable and can be relaid with ease onto the wood base. Use hide (cabinet) glue to hold it in place. Patches on tortoise shell, like burl wood veneers, should be irregular rather than a neat squares or diamond patch. This way they blend into the swirling patterns to be found in the shell.

Marble Badly broken marble-top tables can be rejoined by using an epoxy-resin glue spread thinly on the meeting surfaces. Where the edges have chipped in the join line a mixture of plaster of Paris and pigment colors can be used and arranged to fill the gap.

Modern finishes Lacquers and urethane varnishes are the two most commonly used types these days for finishing furniture. The latter is particularly suited to the small workshop since its application provides a heat-, water- and spirit-resistant surface. Cellulose and tung-oil finishes may also be found.

The preparation of surfaces prior to using these finishes is basically the same as that used in antique restoration. A few differences occur in that staining and ground repairs are sometimes best carried out after a thinned first coat. You might also find that you have an easier job getting a smooth surface since you do not have to worry about destroying the patination through extensive sanding.

In all cases the success of the operation depends on how closely you follow the manufacturer's instructions. The appropriate fillers and recommended stains have to be used. Water-based stains, for example, work best with the lacquer finish since it tends to dissolve other types and cause them to bleed into the finish, producing a murky and obscuring effect.

Acid-catalyzed lacquers and urethane varnishes will give a high gloss finish through being applied with the brush. The standard practice is to thin the first coat in a 20 to 80 percent ratio of thinner to varnish. Once this is dry, sand it with fine garnet paper or steel wool and then stain. Unlike old wood which has a broken color effect, the technique here aims for a really smooth and uniform staining effect.

Cellulose-enamel varnishes, which appeared in the early years of this century, along with some forms of lacquer, are the finishes you are most likely to encounter on the older types of secondhand furniture. Cellulose enamel now forms the main ingredient for the ready-made antiquing kits which have recently become popular. They are similar to the original 'antique finish' employed by the Victorians in that they obscure the grain. This can be helpful if you come across the types of furniture which have been badly stripped or knocked out.

Wax polishing Waxing is the final finish for furniture after the French polish repairs or varnishing of modern pieces has been carried out. Like gluing, it seems to be a simple job but the proper method of continual working brings the wax up to a beautiful shine. The process is similar to French polishing in that by working the wax continuously into the surface with circular movements the solvents evaporate, leaving a thin but durable coat of wax on the surface.

Proprietary waxes can be bought or you can make your own by shredding yellow or brown beeswax and dissolving it in pure turpentine. Use a double boiler, similar to the glue pot, and slowly heat the mixture until it dissolves. For extra hardness and shine carnauba wax can be heated up separately and added to the beeswax mixture. Once finished the wax should have the consistency of a fairly thick cream. Once a piece has been waxed it will not require further attention apart from an occasional wipe with a dry cloth. Further waxings can be made every few months if necessary, but avoid excessive polishing otherwise heavy deposits will form on the wood.

1. A Victorian Louis XV style table, circa 1880.

2. After a dry run to ascertain the order of reassembly, glue together with super glue. Extra glue is injected from the back and mistakes rectified by plunging the join into hot water (80°C). Large fractures are then packed from the back with an epoxy resin and plaster of Paris mixture.

3 and 4. The breccia effect is simulated by filling the holes with untinted plaster. Parts of this are then dug out and colored plaster used.

5. The finished piece.

REUPHOLSTERY

Although belonging to the general category of restoration, reupholstery seems somehow to play second fiddle to wood repairs and renovations. Fabrics have a short life and reupholstery repairs therefore lack the permanence of wood repairs. However, upholstery is responsible for the finished appearance of a piece of seat furniture; if done badly even the finest of chairs will look unsightly and uninteresting, so do take great care.

In the past, upholstery was often considered a more important craft than cabinetmaking. The cabinetmaker was regarded as a manual laborer, while the upholsterer enjoyed a greater social standing as a kind of interior decorator. His opinion was valued by his clients and he was responsible not only for the provision of seat furniture but for all the soft furnishings in a room, such as wall and bed hangings. Certainly these days reupholstery calls for many skills that are not absolutely essential for wood restoration. Much wood restoration is simply a matter of copying and replacing what is missing. Reupholstering a chair involves not only a good eye for design but the sculptor's and engineer's ability to assess how much stuffing, webbing tension and the like are required to make the piece look good, be comfortable and retain its shape after constant use. As a 'working material,' upholstery has to be done well – it is pointless if the finished piece starts to sag and go lumpy after a few days, no matter how good it looked originally!

Below: An upholstered arm chair, circa *1760*.

A brief history of upholstery

Today comfort is expected in seat furniture, so it is hard to realize that until the 1800s, upholstery was always considered a luxury rather than a necessity. In the seventeenth and eighteenth centuries most people made do with a hard wooden seat or rushing, and it was only the well-to-do who could afford the comforts of fully upholstered pieces. The production of fabrics and cloths was an expensive business and it was not until the industrialization of the textile industry on a large scale in the 1800s that fully upholstered furniture was available to a broader spectrum of the public.

The standard method for upholstery throughout the 1700s was the stuffed-over seat. Strips of webbing were tacked to the top of the bare-wood seat rails and these were covered with a piece of burlap. The padding, curled horse hair, was then stitched with string to the burlap to hold it secure and then covered once again with burlap. In most cases the sitter's weight had the greatest effect on the front of the seat rail, so to strengthen it and prevent the collapse of the padding, an extra roll of hair was sewn to the front of the chair. The whole seat was then covered with an underlayer of fine muslin or linen and finally finished off with the top fabric.

The drop-in or insert seat which appeared in the late seventeenth century in England was upholstered in much the same manner as the stuffed-over seat. It was cheaper than the stuffed-over seat as the seat frame was removable from the chair. Consequently it was not so time-consuming to reupholster or re-cover at a later date.

The above two upholstery methods varied slightly in the number of layers of material and different sorts of padding employed but it was not until the Victorian period that a radical change occurred in upholstery techniques – the introduction of springs. So great was the Victorian desire for a comfortable chair that esthetic considerations were disregarded. In order to accommodate these large springs,

chairs inevitably became deeper in the seat and back, and the webbing was attached to the underside of the seat rail as opposed to the top. Upholstered pieces from the mid- and late Victorian period have that lumpy and heavy look, and there is rarely the careful balance of exposed wood and material that is found in eighteenth-century pieces. The upholstery itself dominates the whole effect of Victorian pieces.

The Victorian method of 'overstuffed' upholstery continued through the Edwardian Period, although many of the excesses of the previous generation were curbed. It was at this date that the club-type chair became popular.

A host of new techniques and materials have now replaced the traditional and Victorian methods of upholstery. The flax-based webbing used as a support for the stuffing and springs has now been ousted in favor of the more durable metal-supported springs or, more recently, the introduction of helical or zig-zag springs (also known as 'Z' and ripple-wire springs). Plywood bases to drop-in seats have dispensed with the need for webbing as well and, where it is still used, it is usually made from toughened rubber.

Buying upholstered furniture

Upholstery can sometimes make it difficult to ascertain just how sound a piece is underneath all the material. Three basic steps should be taken before buying what could well be a time-consuming repair job.

One/Check for woodworm. Although the visible parts of many upholstered pieces are made from woods like mahogany which are free from woodworm attack, internal and nonvisible structures of chairs are usually constructed in beech or birch. The furniture beetle thrives on these two woods, so it is important to check that the hidden timber is sound. The only way to do this is to turn the piece upside down and remove a corner of the cambric cloth that covers the bottom. A few holes are not disastrous but where heavy attack is evident and woodworm dust is thick it is best to avoid the piece, unless you want to get involved in a long carpentry job.

Two/Thickness of the wood. Unlike the cabinetmaker whose quality of work is readily apparent, the chairmaker sometimes took shortcuts, knowing that his shoddy workmanship was going to be hidden by the upholstery. Quite often when you strip a chair down to the carcass you will find that the whole structure is made up from thin scraps of timber strengthened by strips of softwood nailed to the seat rails. The only way to test for such deficiencies in a potential purchase is to feel through the cloth to find out whether each component is made from one stout and solid piece of timber. The rails of a stuffed-over seat should be at least 3 inches deep by $1\frac{1}{2}$ inches wide and on the fully upholstered piece 2×2 inches is a good thickness.

Three/Soundness of joints. Most joints in an upholstered chair can come loose or snap off in their housings without the piece actually falling apart. Webbing, material and the like will hold a piece together so that unless you test it to find out, a chair can look perfectly sound when in fact its structure is in a sorry state. The best method for checking is to stand the piece on each of its four legs in turn and gently press down on the leg from the diametrically opposite corner. A slight 'give' indicates that the joint has come loose in its housing. If there is considerable leeway, probably the joint has snapped and will need replacing.

Removing existing materials

A particularly fascinating part of reupholstery is what is known in the trade as 'ripping off.' The removal of all the layers from Victorian and Edwardian furniture is rather like catching a glimpse of the past. Such types provide an interesting illustration of old upholstery techniques so it is useful to have a notebook to record the techniques and layer systems used.

Using the mallet and ripping tool, remove all the holding tacks from the fabric and wood carefully place the edge of the ripping tool against each tack in turn and then drive the tack out of the wood. Work in the direction of the grain, that is, along the seat rails, to avoid splitting the wood. Lay your materials in the order of removal and do not throw anything away at this stage. Even badly damaged materials can be used as a rough template for cutting out new coverings and undercoverings.

Once you reach the bare frame, carefully check for any remaining tacks, signs of woodworm and broken joints. It is best to fix these at this stage and if you have any staining to do, do it now to avoid marking your new materials.

Below: Removing materials from a chair. The tool is always worked in the direction of the grain so that the tacks can be pulled out neatly, without splitting the wood.

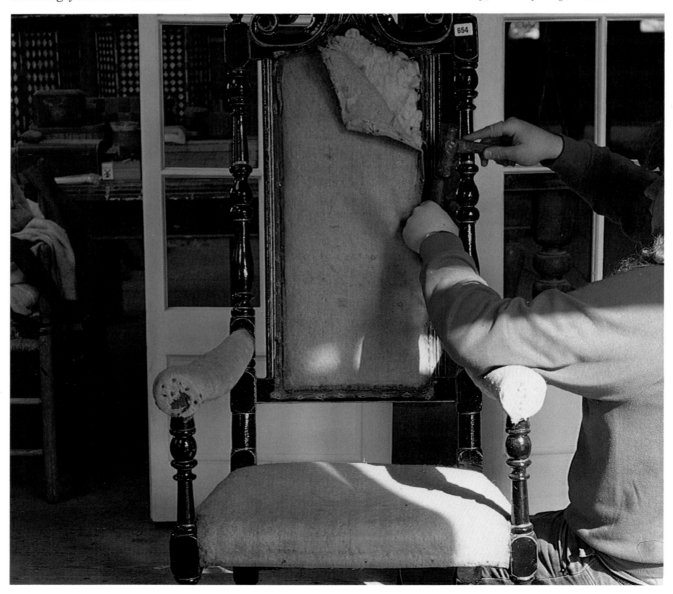

The drop-in seat

The drop-in or insert seat is the easiest of all types to reupholster. It is certainly a good starting point for the beginner. The two most common types are the old webbing and horsehair type and the modern plywood-based frame which uses foam rubber or wadding as its main padding.

Webbed drop-in seat

One/RIPPING OFF When the webbing breaks in these types you have to remove all the material to get at the frame since the strips are placed directly under the stuffing and cannot be replaced from the base. With the seat held firmly in the vise, remove all the materials, tacks and stuffing and then check that the frame is sound and has not warped. Before commencing work take your new undercovering and top material and wrap them around the frame. Now check to see whether the seat will still fit in its recess. Nothing is more infuriating than to find after you have finished the job that the seat will not fit back.

Two/REWEBBING With the seat clamped to the workbench or table proceed to apply the webbing. For the average size drop-in seat two strips across and three from side to side are ample. Use the web stretcher for extra pull and avoid cutting the webbing until after it has been fixed down. Tack down the loose end of the webbing by doubling the strip under itself and remember to stagger the line of the tacks so as not to open a crack in the grain. While you pull with the stretcher, tack the other end, cut off the surplus, fold it over and retack. Six tacks for each end of webbing is ample.

Three/COVERING THE WEBBING To provide a base for the horsehair a layer of burlap is now fixed on top. This should have an inch spare all around which can be folded down and tacked. This layer has to be fairly taut – tack the front, proceed to the back and then finish off with the sides by using a tack every 1½ inches.

Four/PLACING AND FIXING THE STUFFING Horsehair is the standard material but occasionally you will find it mixed with flock. Tease out the existing stuffing or replace it if beyond salvage. Most paddings of this nature compress to one-third of their thickness

1. Ripping off existing fabrics.
2. Rewebbing the frame of the drop-in seat. The web stretcher maintains the correct tension, and the front-to-back webbing is replaced first. The side to side is then interwoven. Note that the edges of the wood were originally chamfered to give a better finishing shape.
3. A layer of burlap is stretched and tacked. Two scraps of wood can be glued with epoxy resin to the jaws of locking jaw pliers to give an even pull (these can be tapped free later).
4. Twine is sewn in rows and horsehair fed under.
5. A good depth of hair is placed onto the locking rows beneath, its shape gauged and its mass distributed evenly.
6. The shape is worked by temporarily tacking the center of each edge and working outward toward the corners. The arrows indicate how one hand pulls the calico in a smoothing action while the other takes up the slack. One hand is then free to reach for the hammer and tack.
7. The corners are pulled (left) and then folded (right) prior to tacking.

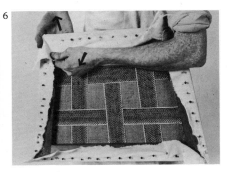

8. Applying the second padding.
9. The top covering. The right-hand side shows how the corner pleat is made and tacked. The left-hand side illustrates how the material is cut up to the nail.
10. The top left-hand corner shows the first fold. The top right corner shows the second fold before the excess material is cut off.
11. The seat returned to the Victorian 'Chippendale' chair.

8
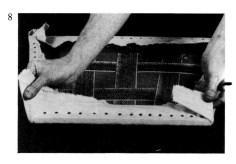

9

10

11

so for the average drop-in seat you will need about a 6-inch thickness of teased-out hair. To prevent the stuffing from shifting, a series of shallow loops should be sewn into the webbing with twine and a semicircular needle. Tuck several small rows of horsehair underneath these. These in turn will lock into the rest of the horsehair and prevent the whole mass from working to the back of the seat with constant use.

Five/UNDERCOVERING This is the crucial part to achieve a uniform and well-balanced shape to the seat. Cut a muslin or calico cloth so that there is ample to spare all round. Temporarily tack the cloth over the horsehair to see how the seat will eventually appear. Redistribute the stuffing if it looks unbalanced and add more to any hollows you find when you run your hand over the material. By gradually smoothing the padding tight work out from the center of the seat toward the edges, retacking as you go to take up the slack material. You will need only three or four tacks per edge and one for each corner at this stage. Once the material is nice and firm tack the edges permanently but leave the corners free. These can now be pleated as illustrated and the surplus material cut away from the base.

Six/SECOND PADDING If you have used curly horsehair as your stuffing a layer of thin wadding or cotton padding should now be placed on the undercover to prevent the horsehair from working its way through. This has to be a sheet so as to provide a uniform effect to the chair once the top cover is fixed in place.

Seven/FINISHING FABRIC By marking the centers of the four edges of the seat you will be able to lay your top material so that its weave is exactly in line with the sides and front of the seat. Allow a good 2-inch overlap under the seat and trim off the excess once you have finished tacking. The corners should be cut, tacked and folded as illustrated.

Plywood-based drop-in seat

This is the alternative method used on modern pieces for the insert seat. As webbing is not durable, early in this century plywood began to replace it. Often these seats are fastened to the chair with screws and these have to be removed to pull the seat clear. Once the seat is stripped down you will probably find that cotton padding has been used as the infill. Occasionally this can be reused but it is often better to replace with a 2-inch thickness of foam rubber.

One/CUTTING THE FOAM TO SHAPE Lay your plywood base on top of the foam and use it as a template to cut the foam to the exact pattern. The long kitchen knife or 7-inch shears can be used for this purpose. Once you have the outline, taper the edges to get a nice rounded shape. Use the scissors and cut at an angle of 45 degrees so that the seat tapers away.

Two/POSITIONING THE FOAM You can use one of two methods. The first is to lay the foam so that its bevel edges face downward into the chair seat. This way, when the fabric is stretched taut it will pull the bevels to the flat to give you a nicely rounded shape. The second is to have the bevel facing up and to trim up the edges into the dome shape.

Three/TOP COVER You rarely need an undercovering material for this type of padding so it is simply a matter of using the existing fabric as a guide to cutting your top cover. This should be stapled to the underside leaving a 3-inch gap before each corner.

Four/FOLDING CORNERS OVER By cutting out the excess material from the corners as illustrated they can then be folded and stapled down. The material should stop about 1½ inches from the edge. Once stapled, the seat can be returned to the chair.

Pin-cushion seat

This is a type of low padded seat which is fixed permanently to the chair frame. As a method it was popular during the Edwardian period for elegant hall and dining chairs.

One/REWEBBING The majority of types are fairly small so you will need only a 3 and 2 arrangement of webbing. This is tacked to the top of the flat chair rails so that it just sits into the shallow recess without affecting the surrounding and finished wood.

Two/WEB COVER A piece of hessian or burlap can be tacked around the frame to cover the webbing. Its edges should be folded under to prevent fraying.

Three/PADDING A small amount of padding is required. Horse-hair covered with a layer of wadding is a good system, though packed cotton fill can also be used. Do not forget to fix the padding to the webbing with stitches. Even on a small seat it will work its way to the back if this is forgotten.

Four/UNDERCOVERING A thin but strong muslin cloth should be used. Measure the exact shape of the seat and allow an inch overlap. Half an inch of this overlap should be folded under itself and the material laid on the chair. On this type of chair you have to tack the back first; if you leave it to the last stages it can be difficult to get the hammer in place because the back of the chair will be in the way. Pull the material to the front, tack it down and proceed to the sides. You might have to use the regulator at this stage to redistribute the stuffing before finally tacking.

Five/TOP COVERING As before, tack the back edge first. With these shallow-seated chairs it is best to use a thin top cover to avoid too much bulk.

Six/EDGING WITH GIMP Once the top cover is on you will see that the tacks are still showing around the edges. These should be covered with a gimp that matches your finishing fabric. Measure the edges of the seat and use one continuous length of gimp, folding the edges as illustrated. This should be glued and lightly pinned in place.

Stuffed seat

This type of seat is based around the traditional eighteenth-century methods, that is, it is a chair without springs. Stages 1–3 show how the webbing is tacked, interlaced and folded over. Remember to fold the loose end of the webbing under itself in the first fixing, whereas in the second fixing it has to be doubled over and tacked down. The common arrangement is 5 strips of webbing but on the larger chairs 3 and 3 and even 4 and 4 should be used.

Stage 4 shows how the webbing cover is tacked down to the frame. On the original covering you might find that this material is reusable, being a tough hessian type. It is secured in the usual fashion by folding the edges under. Note that where it meets the corners part of it has to be cut away to allow for these projections.

The seat can now be padded with any of the materials mentioned. Avoid using foam rubber as it is not in keeping with this type of chair. If ordinary flock or cotton padding is used it should be teased between the fingers and distributed on the seat so that there is more at the center than the sides. This will give you the desired curve to the finished seat.

1. The first strip of webbing is applied to the pin-cushion seat.
2. The end of the webbing is folded over and tacked.
3. (Overleaf) The webbing, interlaced and complete.
4. Tacking on the burlap.
5. Having sewn the stuffing in place (see drop-in seat) the undercover is applied.
6. A second padding and top cover is tacked in place.
7. The top cover tacked and ready for the gimp.
8. The gimp is glued and nailed with pins to finish and hide the tacks.

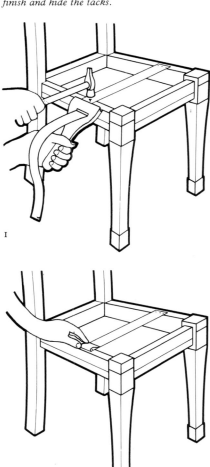

1

2

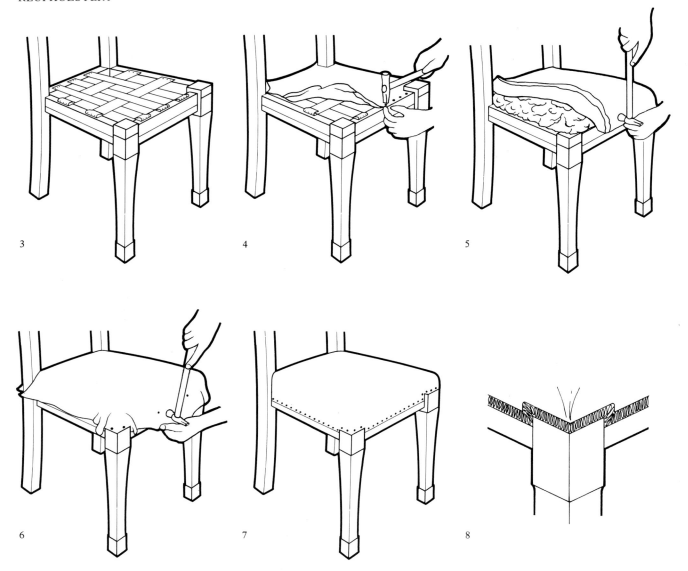

3   4   5

6   7   8

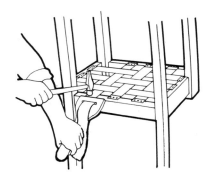

Chair seat with springs: 1. Rewebbing.

Stage 5 The padding is covered with hessian, muslin or scrim and tacked down over the sides to the wooden frame. It is best to stop slightly short of the polished wood so that when the edging gimp is applied it will cover the tacks of the top cover. As usual, check to ensure that the padding is distributed evenly before the final fixing.

Stage 6 The top cover must be cut so that there is sufficient overhang on all four sides. If you have the original, use it as a pattern. First fix the front with a few tacks, then the back and sides. Neatly pleat the corners as illustrated or simply fold the material once so that only one line shows.

Stage 7 shows the piece ready for gimping. In the detail in stage 8 the gimp should be carefully worked around the edge and folded by the method used on the pin-cushion seat.

Chair seat with springs

In this type of chair the webbing is applied to the bottom of the frame as opposed to the top. (*See stage 1.*) If you are reupholstering this sort of chair do check that it was originally fitted with springs. Tack marks on top of the seat rail indicate the simple stuffed chair. Where corner blocks as opposed to corner braces have been used, this usually means that springs were originally employed, corner braces were

2. Sewing in the springs.

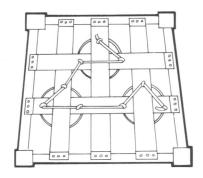

3. Arrangement for 3 springs (from below).

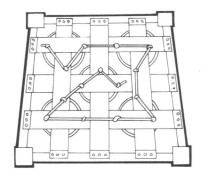

4. Arrangement for five springs (from below).

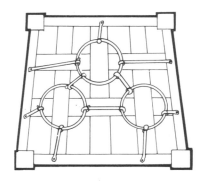

5. Securing three springs (from above).

used where it was not necessary to keep the center of the chair free for the springs.

Turn your chair upside down on some trestles or the workbench in order to facilitate webbing. A webbing cover is not necessary and the springs can be sewn straight into the strips. On small chairs where a 3 and 2 webbing system is used only 3 springs are required – 2 in front and one behind. They should be sewn into the webbing with one length of twine and a semicircular needle or spring needle as illustrated in the worm's eye view in stage 3. Stitch each spring in 3 places and knot as you go. On larger chair seats, 6 pieces of webbing are used and 5 springs sewn in to the intersections. The springs should be positioned so that the finishing end of the coils all point in the same direction.

Before the spring canvas can be applied the springs have to be lashed together and fixed with string to the wooden sides of the chair, Stages 5 and 6 show a bird's eye view of the different arrangements for the 3- and 5-spring arrangement. On the average chair a 6-inch long spring is adequate. Allowing for $1\frac{1}{2}$ inches of padding the springs now have to be pulled down by the same amount, that is compressed by $1\frac{1}{2}$ inches. Stage 7 shows a side view of the springs before tightening (there are 5 springs, the 2 at the far edge of the chair have been removed from the drawing for reasons of clarity). Punch your tacks halfway into the wood and gradually pull the springs down to the required level by feeding the string under the tack and then knotting it at the required length. It is imperative at this stage to compress the springs so that their upper surfaces form a curve. The edge of the spring away from the center of the chair should dip down toward the edges of the chair. Each spring has to be lashed so that it exerts pressure in the same line as its length. If this is not done the spring will push sideways from its center when the chair is used.

By compressing the springs in this way before the padding layer the seat will return to its original shape even after constant use. Once you feel you have a good basis for the finishing shape drive your tacks home, leaving $\frac{1}{2}$ an inch of twine spare. This will stop the stringing fraying close to the tack and consequently coming loose.

Stage 8 shows how the springs are now covered with the spring canvas (heavyweight burlap and hessian). The back edge has to be tacked down first with a few temporary tacks. The canvas is then pulled to the front of the chair and tacked to the rail. The sides should now be tacked alternately starting at the back on one side and so on until it is fixed all round. Try to avoid compressing the springs even further at this stage. The burlap should be tight but not to a degree where it forces the springs down.

The springs can now be sewn into the canvas with the spring needle. Use one length of twine and proceed in the same manner as described in stages 3 and 4, knotting each spring as you go (stage 9). In this case try to end up with your last knot in the same place as the starting point.

The padding should now be applied (Stage 10). Tease it out to the required shape and amount, remove it from the chair and proceed to stitch a fastening into the spring canvas to act as a fixing for the padding. Use a medium-grade twine and start about 3 inches up from the chair frame, working around in a square and loosely stitching every 4 inches. Once this is done feed bits of hair under these ties and then pull the whole length of string tight. You should now have an open square of padding into which the remainder can be packed as evenly as possible.

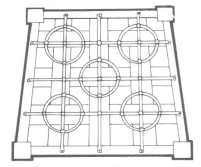

6. Securing five springs (from above).

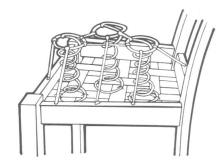

7. Side view of springs secured and ready to be tightened to form the dome.

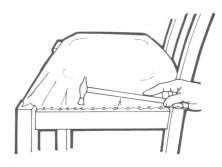

8. Tacking on the burlap spring canvas.

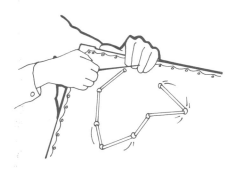

9. Securing the springs to the burlap.

Use an open-weave cloth such as the scrim type and place it centrally over the stuffing. Temporarily tack the edges of the cloth to the side frames. Stitch another square line above the previous one with a straight 8-inch mattress needle. This secures your sandwich of spring canvas and scrim, with its filling of stuffing, together. This operation is particularly difficult and it is essential that you use a long double-pointed needle. Push the needle through the sandwich and pull it out from the other side between the webbing. Now move along 3 inches and punch the needle back up to the top surface. Pull it clear from the top, move along another three inches on your square and then push the needle back down again. Continue in this fashion to form the square. Once done the string can be pulled tightly to lock the whole sandwich together. The springs and webbing are totally irrelevant at this stage, so avoid catching the needle and sewing them to the spring canvas.

Now remove your temporary tacks which hold the edges of the scrim and add more stuffing so that the scrim protrudes slightly beyond the edge of the frame. This will provide the extra material needed to form the roll edge. With the edge of the scrim folded under itself, it can now be tacked to the edges of the frame. Do not pull it too tight as you will need a bit of give for the roll edge. Stage 11 shows the tacking process.

Blind stitching Thread your needle and, starting about 2 inches from the back corner and just above the tacks, push it upward at an angle of 45 degrees toward the top so that it emerges 2 inches from the edge of the seat. Do not pull the needle out; stop just before the eye appears. Twist the needle in your fingers and then push it down again at the same angle of 45 degrees so that it emerges through the side of the scrim about 2 inches along from your starting point at the back edge of the chair. Now take your thread back to your original starting point, knot it and then move along a further two inches, parallel with the tacks, insert the needle and then proceed to make another V stitch up to the top of the scrim at an angle of 45 degrees. Push the needle down again so that it emerges at the starting point and loop the twine around the base three times before proceeding to the next stitch. Stage 12 shows how this is done. Once you have completed one edge pull the twine tight so that the stuffing is forced toward the edge. Continue with the remaining edges of the chair in this manner and, finally, knot once everything is tight.

Stitching the roll edge As shown in stage 13 the roll edge now has to be made. A similar stitch is used to that of the blind stitch but in this case a series of parallel stitches are used and the needle taken through and out of the scrim cover. Stage 14 shows how the stitching should be done. Start in one corner at the back of the seat, place the needle at an angle into the scrim about 1 inch above the blind stitching and then push it up so that it emerges about 1 inch from the top edge. Move along one inch and push the needle down again so as to form a series of parallel stitches as shown in stage 14.

Once the roll edge is finished you can cover the chair but a better effect can be achieved by applying a second stuffing of horse hair, wadding or similar material. Whatever you use should be sewn in such a way that the stuffing will not shift or work into lumps. Proceed to stitch in a series of loose ties about 2 inches in from the edge. Under these can be tucked parts of your second stuffing, before the center is completely filled.

Before applying the undercovering material the corners of the chair can be fitted with a thin framing of cardboard to give them a clearly

10. Placing the padding.

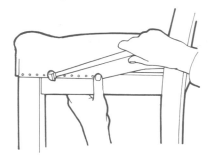

11. Tacking on the padding cover.

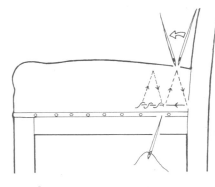

12. Blind stitching.

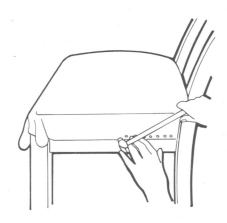

15. Undercovering.

defined shape. These should finish a little distance below the upper surface of the stuffing and the edges rounded so as not to reveal any marked angles.

The second stuffing can now be covered with unbleached calico or muslin and the corners tucked in in the usual fashion (stage 15). A thin layer of batting or cotton sheet has to be laid on top of the calico at this stage, particularly if you have used horsehair for the second stuffing. The chair can now be covered with your finishing fabric.

All that remains to be done is to apply the bottom dust cloth as shown in stage 16 and to apply the gimp edging to hide the tacks (stage 17).

Rewebbing a sprung chair Quite often the chair with springs only requires rewebbing to put it back into service. Turn the chair over and remove the dust cloth to reveal the snapped webbing. Cut all the stitches that secure the springs to the webs and then remove the webbing with your ripping tool. The springs at this stage will shoot up higher than the base and you will have to feed your webbing through them in order to tack it down. Tack in your back to front webbing first, then push the springs under this and then proceed with the side to side strips. Remember to interweave them. You will need to pull the webbing very tight as the springs will force them out. Once the webbing is complete, center the springs on the intersections and stitch them in place by the methods already described. Replace the base cloth and tack as usual.

The above types of chair and the methods used only really scrape the surface of all the techniques used in upholstery. For further information the reader should consult books that deal solely with upholstery or, better still, enroll in evening classes. A more ambitious undertaking such as the fully upholstered and buttoned type of chair requires detailed instructions if it is to be done properly.

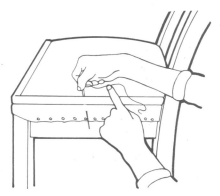

13. Stitching the roll edge.

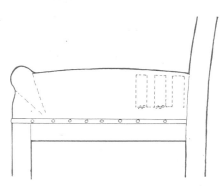

14. Roll stitching method.

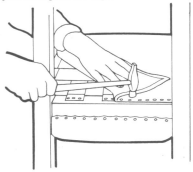

16. Tacking on the dust cover.

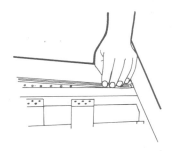

17. Applying the gimp.

CANING, RUSHING and WICKER

Caning provides a cheap and attractive way of seating a chair. The material, a type of split rattan, was first imported into Europe from Malaysia in the mid-seventeenth century. By the 1670s in London it had become so popular as a cheap alternative to upholstery, that the upholsterer's guild tried to have the craft suppressed. They were unsuccessful and it continued to be popular at various periods right up to the present day. Most of the chairs you are likely to encounter will date from the Edwardian period or a little later. Earlier examples can be found dating mainly from the periods between 1665–1740 and 1770–1840, but these are quite rare and can be very valuable.

If you are trying caning for the first time you should bear in mind the following points and general techniques.

One/As a beginner it takes a whole day to cane a small chair. It is not a particularly comfortable occupation as your hands have to be constantly wet and they can get cut by the cane. There is no real way to protect them apart from applying a barrier cream. Unfortunately, gloves cannot be worn as it is a very delicate job.

Two/Throughout the process the cane lengths have to be kept moist. A basin of cold water should be placed within your reach so as to extract the cane as you need it. It is best to soak the first 3 lengths of cane half an hour before you start and while you are stripping the old cane off the chair. As you take a wet length out replace it with a new one from your dry bundle.

Three/The shiny side of the cane should be used with its *face uppermost* during the whole operation, even under the seat rails. Try to avoid twisting the cane and keep the dull side flat against the wood, both on the surface and through the holes.

Four/You will find that you run out of a length from time to time. Use the method of joining illustrated. Here you will probably have to resoak the end and previous loop to make the cane supple enough to allow three twists. If your cane runs out in the middle of the chair, temporarily peg the nearest hole and join your new length to the nearest finished loop under the frame.

Five/Do not pull the cane too tight. Initially in the first three stages the rows should have a slight 'give' when you press them down.

Six/Never try to economize by using a cane which has a weak spot. Go back to the nearest fixing point and join in a new length as illustrated.

Seven/Before starting work, count the holes on the front, back and sides and then mark your center holes. On circular and fancy seats make a taut cross in the center of the chair by pegging in two bits of string running from these holes from side to side and back to front. With a protractor or by simply using your eye check that the intersections of the string are an exact right angle all round and that the strings mark the exact center of the seat. On fancy shapes this is essential, as the cane will fan out from your center in a uniform pattern. On circular or semicircular chairs you might have to move your center hole to the left or right to produce this right angle in the center. On the standard square chair the counting method is probably all you will have to use.

Eight/If you are lucky enough to find original cane work on late seventeenth- and early eighteenth-century pieces, try to restore only

Right : A late-17th-century beechwood chair, upholstered in about 1850. It is painted with modern black and gold paint.
Below: The chair stripped of its upholstery and paint to show the original cane back. Note that the front stretcher to the legs has been removed. This was a later replacement in oak and a new one should be carved in beech to match the top cresting rail. Both the ends of the arms had been sawn off in the Victorian period in order to fit the square ends for the padding. Vestiges of a thin coat of gesso simulated with walnut grain were found under the upholstery.

Despite the fact that this chair is nearly 300 years old, it is badly designed and made. The use of thin uprights, particularly in beech, means that the tall backs of such chairs often break off.

the broken strands rather than ripping out the whole sheet. Examples from this period are extremely rare. It is possible to cut out the broken strands, splice in a new length and reweave.

Nine/The art of caning depends on touch as much as sight. The finished piece should feel as good as it looks. Blind people do some really superb caning just by touch.

Materials and tools Bundles of cane can be purchased from most craft shops or workshops. The sizes you will need are No 2, No 4 and No 6. You can economize by using the No 2 size only for the whole chair but a better effect can be achieved with the three different widths. Two types of pegs are required. The first is used for temporarily pegging and can either be some golf tees or bits of $\frac{1}{4}$-inch dowelling chamfered to a taper with a craft knife and smoothed with sandpaper. The second type are the ones that go in permanently in the finishing stages – basket cane is the traditional material, being made from the inner portion or pith of the rattan cane. If you cannot get hold of any basket cane, use No 3 or No 4.

Few tools are needed for caning. A blunt-ended bradawl or knitting needle with its point rounded can be used to push the basket cane out of the holes, and as a feeder for the new cane. A hammer and a pair of point-nose pliers are handy. The former can be used for tapping the looped joins flat while the pliers can help in removing the old cane lengths from the holes. Lastly, a good-quality craft knife fitted with a new blade is needed.

Preparation Cut a large area of broken cane seat from your chair and lay it to one side in case you need it for reference. Pull or push the old pegs out of the holes with the pliers and bradawl. In some chairs the pegs come out easily if pushed from underneath. Once the chair is free of all its old cane, check the holes and do any necessary carpentry repairs, staining and polishing before beginning the caning.

The seven-step process below is called the standard double setting. This produces six layers of cane. Steps 1–3 involve no weaving. The cane size is shown at the beginning of each step.

STEP 1. No 2 width cane. You can either start at the edge of the chair having counted the respective amount of holes away from the center

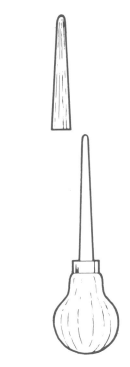

Top: Method of joining new lengths.
Above: Bradawl and basket cane peg.

Left: Old basket cane pegs can be removed easily if you can tell from which direction they were originally pegged. It is then a simple matter of pushing each alternate hole upward or downward as the case may be.

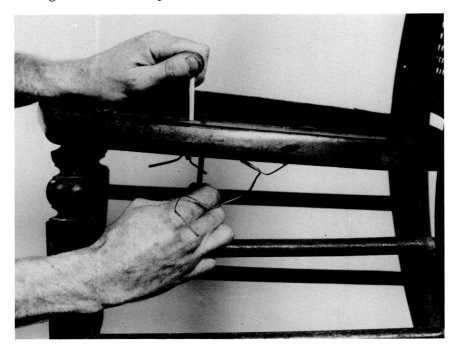

Right: The six stages of caning. The best effect can be achieved by using No 2 cane for the first four steps and No 4 cane for the last two.

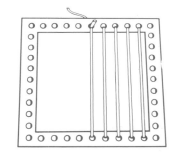

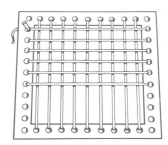

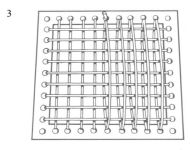

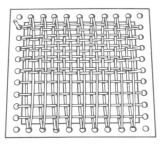

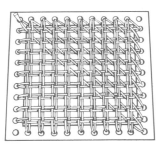

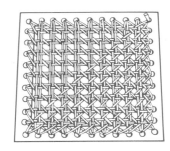

mark or begin in the middle. The latter is easier for the beginner as it involves a simplified two-step process. Thread your cane up through the center back hole, leave about 4 inches hanging free and temporarily peg it with your dowel or tee. Take the length to the marked front center hole, pass it down and through, keeping the glossy side uppermost. Pull up through the next hole and feed the cane back to the back rail. Once you have reached the edge, temporarily peg the last hole and leave the requisite 4 inches of spare cane. Place a dry length of cane into your basin and with the next strand of wetted cane start to the left of the front hole. Peg and then carry on filling in the left-hand side in the same fashion.

STEP 2. No 2 cane. Leaving the corner hole free, start from the back left-hand corner of the side rail and proceed to work toward the front by laying these layers horizontally on top of the vertical lengths. Feed the strips through the holes in exactly the same fashion as step 1 and fill in the whole frame, stopping short of the right-hand corner hole. Temporarily peg, as usual.

STEP 3. No 2 cane. This stage is a simple repeat of step one. Fill in the right-hand side, starting from the center hole. Work from front to back, laying the cane on top of the previous vertical strands to form a 'sandwich' with the horizontals as the 'filling'. While these new vertical strands should lie on top of step one strands, it can help to push them slightly to the right. This has been exaggerated and the strips bowed in the drawing for purposes of clarity. Now complete the left-hand side. Place a strip of No 4 cane in your basin at this stage.

STEP 4. No 2 cane. Now proceed to add the partner to the horizontal strands executed in step 2. This is the first stage of weaving. Start again at the hole nearest the corner one as in step 2 and weave the cane under the first strand and over the second strand in each vertical pair. On the next row, as you work back across to the left, weave it over and then under the vertical lengths. Proceed to fill the whole frame in this manner. It can help to weave about 6 verticals before pulling your strand through.

STEP 5. No 4 cane. Taking your soaked No 4 proceed to sharpen the threading end with your craft knife. Taper the point right back without making it too flexible. This will help you enormously in threading the cane through the holes which will be starting to fill up at this stage. Carry on sharpening your new lengths from now on. Pass the length up through the top left-hand hole at the back of the chair, this has been unused so far. Weave the cane diagonally toward the front right-hand hole, passing under the vertical and over the horizontal pairs. Once you reach the corner, feed the sharpened point down and up through the first hole from the corner hole in the right-hand frame of the chair. Now work back, weaving as you go, and keeping your new strand parallel with the first diagonal. Fill in the top right-hand triangle. Now using the same corner holes twice, start at the back left-hand corner and weave diagonally as before until you reach the right-hand front hole as shown. Complete the other triangle.

STEP 6. No 4 cane. This step forms the opposite diagonal. Start at the back right-hand corner hole feeding the cane up through it as usual. Weave in a reversed fashion to step 5, that is under the horizontal and over the vertical pairs. Fill one half of the frame and, using the same corner hole twice, complete the other half. You might find you will have to clear the holes with your bradawl or needle at this stage, but do watch out about damaging the cane in these holes. While it is best to tie up your new lengths to the nearest loop as you proceed through the process, you might find that you have still got some temporary pegs securing the cane. Tie the loose ends up underneath and proceed to put on the border.

STEP 7. Nos 2 and 6. This is the stage where a border of No 6 is whipped into the edge to protect the cane edge from wear. First of all permanently peg every second hole, leaving the corner free. Push one end of the No 6 into the front left-hand corner hole and temporarily peg it in place. Take this length across the front rail and push it into the right-hand corner hole. Now take your No 2 up through the nearest unplugged hole to the front left-hand corner hole (this should be the third hole along, working from left to right), pass it over the wider No 6 and back down through the same hole. Remember to keep the shiny side uppermost on these canes. Continue to whip the cane down in this fashion using every alternate hole, stopping two holes short of the right-hand corner hole. Tie in your whipping cane underneath and then proceed to repeat the system for the remaining three sides of the chair. Once this is done the chair should be turned upside down, loose ends secured and all the unpegged holes, pegged permanently from the bottom.

TAPERED SEAT On seats like the one illustrated where you find more holes in the front rail than the back, the cane has to be taken through the side rails as shown. Here it is essential to keep an exact parallel as you pass over the wood of the right-hand rail.

Cleaning and preserving cane Avoid chemical cleaners or household detergents. A very mild solution of cold salt water is all that is needed.

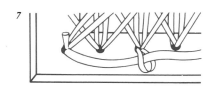

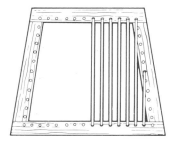

Above: Whipping the edge of the seat with No 6 cane held in place by an over and under arrangement of No 2.

Below: Caning a tapered seat.

Rush-seated chair

Rush has been a popular material for chair seats since the seventeenth century in both Europe and America, particularly for country furniture. It is made by simply twisting lengths of rush, either singly or doubled, and then passing them around the chair frame in a logical pattern. The thinner the rush length is and the more it is twisted, the finer will be the finished seat. Rustic chairs employ thicker strands and less twist to each piece of fiber. You can usually tell what method to use by the way the chair is constructed. On finely rushed pieces which have had their rush removed the chair leg only extends $\frac{1}{4}$ of an inch or less above the rails, so that when the piece is finished the tops of the legs rest in the same plane as the rush. The chair on page 154 is an early nineteenth-century ashwood ladder-back. Note that here the legs extend an inch or more above the rails. This is a sure indication that a 'fatter' type of rush with less twist should be used. The peculiar back chamfering of the seat rails is also a way of telling whether a chair was originally rushed.

Two common varieties of rush can be purchased: ordinary rush (known as green rush) and saltrush which has a golden yellow color. The latter is the better quality but both types can be used. They come in large bundles, in lengths of up to six feet, and you can pick them yourself from marshy areas of land, preferably in the late summer period. However, remember to cut each piece as close to the ground as possible and dry the rushes carefully. Avoid twisting or bending each length.

Soak your lengths of rush, and while waiting for them to become pliable, strip off the old rush. Some types of chairs have a wooden strip nailed round all the edges of the rush between the legs. This has to be prised off and the rush sliced open along the rail. Keep as much of the original as possible intact – it can act as a guide to the method of weaving, knots used and how much twist has been applied to the strands. Remember to twist the rush strands constantly through the process so that you are turning them into a type of rope. If you want a good thick seat then only twist a couple of times as you approach, and leave, each corner. The method of rushing is as follows: take the longest fiber and place the thick end (that is, the root end) alongside the inner edge of rail 4. Now pass the length over and around the front rail (rail 1), over the previous part and around rail 4. This will lock your rush in place and provide a fixing. Pass along under the frame twisting the rush length in your hands from left to right to leg B. Here you use the same arrangement, passing over rail 2, around it over the twisted part and around and under rail 1. Continue up to leg C using exactly the same system, then across to leg D and back down to the left-hand corner (leg 1). By this method of looping over the rails and working in a counterclockwise direction the whole seat eventually fills in.

As the lengths of rush are taken around the frame you will have to add new pieces on. The strongest method is a simple reef knot. A quicker way takes a little practice, as illustrated above, and can eventually be done with the right hand alone. Note that the direction of twist is from left to right and that the twist should not be allowed to get slack.

Once you have completed a few rounds use a wedge-shaped piece of wood (called a packing stick) and line up all the lengths, forcing them together and against the side of the legs. You will see at this stage that a pocket has formed between the top and bottom strands. For extra security and to give a greater fullness to the seat, stuff some

Below: This shows the difference in the amount of twist between the surface rush and the lengths underneath, which run parallel to the rails.
Bottom left and right: These two photos show the difference in twist between the top and bottom of a rush-seated chair.

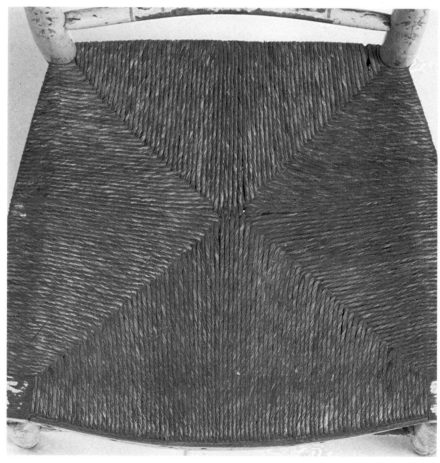

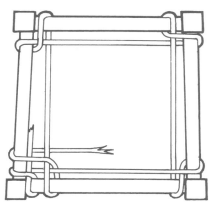

*Above: The process of rushing a seat.
Left: An early-19th-century ashwood ladder back awaiting rushing and showing the chamfering to the rails peculiar to many types of rush-seated chairs.*

Below: The slip-knot and professional-knot method of joining lengths of rush during rushing. Also shown is the decorative effect that can be achieved by twisting different colored rushes together to form a single strand.

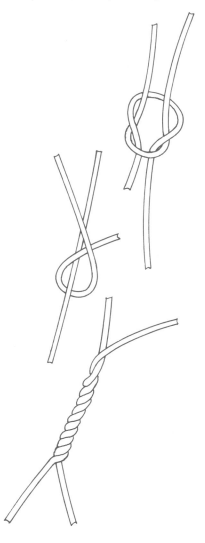

waste strands into the recesses. Carry on in the same fashion until you reach the center, keeping the pockets packed to give a sweep to each of the sections.

SHAPED SEATS Where you find a chair that is wider at the front than the back, one way of bringing the work to an even center is to have a finer twist at the back than at the front in order to make up for the difference between the two rails. When the corners of a section do not come to a point as, for example, on oblong seats, the remainder of the work can be filled in by carrying the strands over one rail and under the next in a figure eight. The rush should still be twisted in these areas.

By combining two lengths of different colored rush together, such as the green and the golden, a decorative effect can be achieved. As with caning it is sometimes possible to restore broken rush strands without having to start from scratch. Pull the broken lengths to the underneath and join a new length on. The new piece should be twisted as described above and pulled through to the top, carried over the frame and then tied with a loop and passed under a few strands on the bottom part of the seat.

The rush over the front part of the chair suffers the greatest wear and tear. Wooden strips are frequently nailed to the outside of the front rail to protect the rush. Be careful not to hit a nail through a strand of rush.

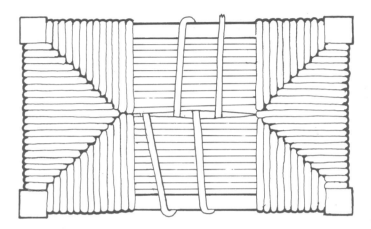

Left: The figure eight method of bringing the work to an even center on oblong seats.

Below: The methods used to join the constructional frames of wicker furniture. The strongest method is to lash the halved joint together with the cane. Very often a rickety chair can be saved by rewhipping these joints with water-soaked No 2 cane.

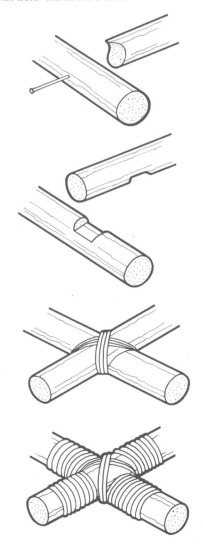

Wicker furniture

Wicker furniture is made by the same process and materials used in basket weaving. The techniques are basically the same so that some forms of chairs are often called basket chairs.

The restoration of wicker furniture can be a little tricky. Most types, garden chairs and so forth, consist of a framework of thick cane or willow rod which is fixed roughly together with nails or woven cane. Often this structure relies partly on the interwoven lattice work of osier rods which is then structured around the frame. The breaking and weakening of the weave causes a kind of chain reaction so that you will often find you can push the top half of the chair in all directions, while it creaks like crazy. Replacing the broken osier rods in the weave often weakens the piece to a certain extent. These rods are the shoots of the willow shrub and though used in the original work it is often better to use a different material. The weave will probably have weakened with age, so if you replace parts with springy new osier, it can force the inner rods to snap. The best material is the more supple pith cane. Select the correct thickness and soak before use. This can then be woven in place so that it dries and conforms to shape without cracking the original.

White wicker work should be washed in a strong solution of salt water and then dried with a cloth. To pull the water out completely choose a sunny day and leave the piece outside. This will also help in the bleaching effect.

Antique wicker work or early twentieth-century pieces command an amazing price, particularly small children's chairs. Do check with a dealer before repairing and cleaning if you have selling in mind. Sometimes they prefer to do the work themselves, or get a professional to do it.

Hot water should never be used to clean wicker, be it old or new. Each piece of osier rod has a natural polish which is part of its strength. The heat will cause the water to penetrate and destroy this. Avoid the use of soaps, household cleaners and sodas as well. Brown wicker furniture is best cleaned by rubbing with a rag dipped in kerosene.

BIBLIOGRAPHY

Repairing furniture

Charles Hayward, *Woodworker's Pocket Book*,
  Evans Brothers Ltd, 1978
Mel Marshall, *How to Repair, Reupholster and
  Refinish Furniture*, Harper & Row, 1979, New York

Restoring furniture

Desmond Gaston, *Care and Repair of Furniture*,
  Collins, London, 1977
Charles Hayward, *Antique Furniture Repairs*, Evans
  Brothers Ltd, 1976
Lorraine Johnson, *How to Restore and Repair
Practically Everything*, Nelson, 1978
George Savage, *The Art & Antique Restorers
  Handbook*, Barrie & Jenkins, London, 1980
Leslie Wenn, *Restoring Antique Furniture*, Barrie &
  Jenkins, London, 1976

Furniture History

James Ayres, *Shell Book of the Home in Britain
  1500–1850*, Faber & Faber, London, 1981
Ralph Fastnedge, *English Furniture Styles 1500–1830*,
  Penguin Books, 1969
Marjorie Filbee, *Dictionary of Country Furniture*,
  Book Club Associates, 1978
Peter Filp, *Furniture of the World*, Cathay Books,
  London, 1974
John Fleming & Hugh Honour, *Penguin Dictionary
  of Decorative Arts*, Penguin
Herbert Gescinsky, *The Gentle Art of Faking
  Furniture*, Dover Publications, New York, 1967
Christopher Gilbert, *Late Georgian and Regency
  Furniture*, Country Life Collectors Guides, 1972
Charles Hayward, *Antique or Fake?*, Evans Brothers
  Ltd, 1979
Edward T Joy, *Chippendale*, Country Life Collectors
  Guides, 1977

Woods

The International Book of Wood, Mitchell Beazley
  Ltd, London, 1979
Bryan Latham, *Timber: A Historical Survey*, Harrap,
  London, 1957

Upholstery

*Golden Age of English Furniture Upholstery 1660–
  1845*, Stable Court Exhibition Galleries, Temple
  Newsam, Leeds, 1973

Lacquer Work

H Koizumi, *Lacquer Work: A Practical Exposition*,
  Pitman, 1923
J S Stalker & G Parker, *A Treatise of Japanning and
  Varnishing*, Oxford, 1688; Tiranti reprint, London
  1971

SOURCES for MATERIALS

Mail Order Suppliers

Fiddes & Son
Trade Street, Cardiff, GB
Specialist suppliers of waxes, stains, chemicals,
polishes and so on for cabinetmaking and restoration

Rustins Limited
Waterloo Road, Cricklewood,
London, NW2 7TX, GB
Wood finishes, paints, thinners and so on

Constantine
2050 Eastchester Road, Bronx, NY 10461, USA
Tools, materials, woods, veneers, stains, cabinet
hardware

Minnesota Woodworkers Supply Company
Industrial Boulevard, Rogers, Minn 55374, USA
Tools, materials, venner, finishes, cabinet hardware

World of Wood, The Art Veneer Co
Industrial Estate, Mildenhall, Suffolk, IP28 7AY, GB
Specialist suppliers of veneer, tools, finishes, handles
and pulls. Worldwide distribution

Craftsman Wood Service Company
2727 South Mary Street, Chicago, ILL 60608, USA
Tools, materials, woods, veneers, hardware

Beardmore
3 Percy Street, London, W1, GB
Reproduction cabinet hardware

Period Furniture Hardware
123 Charles Street, Boston, Mass 02104, USA
Reproduction cabinet hardware

GLUE CHART

Type	Use	Application	Properties and limitations	Solvents and removing agents
Animal.	Antique furniture repairs and hand veneering.	Dissolve in water. Use hot. Surfaces have to be warm. Clamped and rubbed joints. Amber colored.	Amalgamates with old glue. Water soluble. Low resistance to extremes of moisture and heat. Highly stress resistant. Dries amber colored in 24 hours.	Hot water, steam. Blowtorch flame burns it off from coated surfaces.
Casein.	Joinery repairs to old and modern indoor furniture.	White liquid or powder mixed with water. Use cold on both surfaces.	Heat resistant but not totally waterproof. Cannot be used for rubbed joints. Dries white or yellow in 24 hours. Stains some woods.	Hot water and ammonia. Proprietary paint stripper.
Celluloid.	Metal and ivory inlay repairs.	Transparent liquid used from tube. Only coat nonabsorbent surfaces.	Not suitable for large wood repairs. Heat and water resistant. Dries rapidly, goes transparent.	Nail varnish remover. Acetone. Ether. Amyl acetate. Cellulose-paint thinner.
Polyvinyl acetate and aliphatic resin.	Indoor furniture, plastics, rubber, hardboard and so on. Minor repairs to antiques.	White/yellow liquid or cream powder mixed with water. Coat all surfaces. Clamp or rubbed joints.	Versatile. Stress resistant. Poor resistance to heat and moisture. Dries clear in 15 hours but can darken when used on some hardwoods.	Hot water.
Urea and resorcinol.	Indoor and outdoor furniture.	Ready mixed as a white powder miscible in water, or as brown powder to be mixed with liquid. Coat both surfaces. Clamp or rubbed joints.	Stress, moisture and heat resistant. Gap filling qualities. Sets clear or tan colored in 6–12 hours depending on type and conditions.	Occasionally paint stripper.
Epoxy-resin.	Metal, glass, china and so on. Sometimes wood depending on type.	Two part pack. Adhesive and hardener mixed in equal quantities.	Highly stress, moisture and heat resistant. Sets clear or tan. Packing and gap filling qualities. Five-minute or eight-hour setting after mixing. Not suitable for large wood repairs.	Few. Some paint strippers will turn it rubbery.
Contact and impact cement.	Plastic and wood. Veneer to timber.	Ready-to-use liquid. Coat both surfaces and bring into contact after recommended drying period.	Heat, stress and moisture resistant. Sets immediately on contact. Dries clear.	Proprietary thinner.
'Super' glues.	Most nonporous materials. Gesso and compo repairs.	Thin, clear, ready-to-use liquid.	Avoid flesh contact. Bonds in five seconds. Not suitable for wood repairs.	No solvent.

INDEX

Acknowledgments

My special thanks are due to Christopher Gilbert and the staff of Temple Newsam House Museum for teaching me how to view furniture, to my parents for passing on their skills, to Alan and Lindy Ramsden-Hare for workshop and studio facilities, to Ray Gautier for his sheer professionalism, to Lorraine Johnson for starting the ball rolling, to Catharine McDermott for her perception and encouragement, to Jonathan Raisin for his help in the final hours, to Penny Murphy for preparing the index, to Jane Laslett for curbing my natural verbosity and finally to Ruth for – everything.

The author provided all the photographs except for those listed below:

American Museum in Britain pp front cover, 19, 23 (top), 24, 66
Artwork drawn by Smith Brown Associates
Additional artwork by Lorna Turpin
Christies, London pp 1, 10 (right), 14, 17, 23 (below), 25 (both), 86 (left), 99 (right), 134
Design Council pp 7 (both), 28
Victoria and Albert Museum pp 11, 13 (top), 15, 16, 20, 21, 22, 26 (below), 27, 29, 51, 65, 70, 87 (top), 114

Tools and materials supplied by Gillman and son, Smith and Duncan, and Wyard Mattock of Cirencester.

Furniture illustrated: Ramsden-Hare Antiques and Corinium Antiques of Cirencester. Bed of Roses Antiques, Cheltenham. Sir Toby Clarke, Bart. Mr and Mrs Christopher Walsh. Count Juan Sarsfield-Salazar, M.C. Mrs Hermione Morgan, Mr and Mrs Geoffrey Green, Melvyn Boustead, Es Mr and Mrs Ellis Pehkonen, Sir Anth Denny, Bart.